The British experience in India began some 350 years ago, during the reign of Queen Elizabeth I, when a few humble merchants applied for trading concessions from the all-powerful Mogul emperors. From these simple beginnings the British in India became undisputed masters of a vast and teeming subcontinent.

In this book, Dr. Judd tells the history of the British in India, from the first tentative contacts between the East India Company and the Indians to India's final march towards independence, and analyses the social, economic and political consequences of expanding trade, steady conquest and growing administrative burdens. Great personalities and events dominate the story—Robert Clive and Warren Hastings, Curzon, Gandhi and Jinnah; the Battle of Plassey (1757), the Black Hole of Calcutta, and the Indian Mutiny of 1857; the wars along the North-West frontier, the dreadful famine of 1899-1900, the Amritsar massacre, and Gandhi's civil disobedience movement. But above all, the author evokes the complex relationship which developed between the British and the Indians—the rulers and the ruled—and shows how the interaction of these two very different cultures affected peoples' everyday lives.

THE BRITISH RAJ

Denis Judd

WAYLAND PUBLISHERS LONDON

SBN 85340 183 7
Copyright © by Wayland (Publishers) Ltd.
101 Grays Inn Road, London WC1
Photoset and printed by BAS Printers Limited, Wallop, Hampshire

Contents

The Illustrations

＊

1 Beginnings, 1583–1708

THE FIRST MENTION of an Englishman setting foot in India is contained in the *Anglo-Saxon Chronicle*, one of the earliest records of the history of the English. According to this source, King Alfred the Great sent a certain Sighelm on a pilgrimage to India in A.D. 883. Sighelm apparently brought back "many strange and precious unions [pearls] and costly spices (1)." Many centuries before Sighelm and Alfred the Great, the commercial lure of India, and of the trade that crossed its frontiers, was known in Europe. But the spices and exotic goods that poured through India and the Indian Ocean into the insatiable markets of Europe reached the Mediterranean through the prosperous ports of the Levant. European merchants thus had to rely upon middlemen for the supply of commodities that were both desirable and highly profitable.

But by the end of the fifteenth century two European explorers claimed to have found other sea routes to the Indies. Christopher Columbus, who had crossed the Atlantic in 1492, went to his death bed still convinced that he had discovered the Indies. Vasco da Gama, sailing for Portugal in 1497, actually did round the southern tip of Africa, and went on to reach the spice port of Calicut on the Malabar coast of south-western India.

Da Gama's epic voyage fired the imagination, and the commercial hopes, of Europe. The English shared the excitement. "The Indies are discovered," proclaimed a petition sent to the young King Henry VIII in 1511, "and vast treasure brought from thence every day. Let us therefore bend our

11

Opposite Throughout the seventeenth century the Company diversified and extended its trade in India

endeavours thitherwards; and if the Spaniards and the Portuguese suffer us not to join with them, there will be yet region enough for all to enjoy (2)." Poets enriched their work with references to India and the East. Christopher Marlowe, the Elizabethan playwright, wrote (3):

> *Men from the farthest equinoctial line*
> *Have swarmed in troops into the Eastern India,*
> *Lading their ships with gold and precious stones,*
> *And made their spoils . . .*

Marlowe returned to this theme in *Faustus*, who is made to say (4):

> *Shall I make spirits fetch me what I please . . .*
> *I'll have them fly to India for gold,*
> *Ransack the ocean for orient pearl,*
> *And search all corners of the new-found world*
> *For pleasant fruits and princely delicates* [spices].

John Milton wrote in *Paradise Lost* of "Agra and Lahor of Great Mogul (5)."

Father Stevens   But it was not only poetic imaginations that were being stirred. In 1579 an English Jesuit, Thomas Stevens, went to India as Rector of the Jesuit College at Goa, and wrote letters to his father that were widely circulated. Father Stevens showed that not only was India rich in trading possibilities, but that it contained cultural riches as well. Stevens eagerly described the Marathi language, which was widely spoken in west-central India: "Like a jewel among pebbles, like a sapphire among jewels, is the excellence of the Marathi tongue. Like the jasmine among blossoms, the musk among perfumes, the peacock among birds, the Zodiac among the stars, is Marathi among languages (6)."

In 1583 a group of London merchants organized an expedition to India. Ralph Fitch, William Leeds and James Story set sail in the *Tyger*. After landing at Tripoli in North Africa they followed the overland route to India. Later, Fitch sang the praises of what he had seen: "Here is great traffic for all sorts of spices and drugs, silk and cloth of silk, elephants teeth and much China work, and much sugar which is made of

The founding of the Company that was to lead to British dominion in India—the East India Company was granted a charter by Queen Elizabeth in 1600

the nut called 'Gajara'; the tree is called the palmer: which is the profitablest tree in the world (7)."

Under pressure from the English merchants—and hoping for vast customs dues from direct trade with the East—Queen Elizabeth I granted in December, 1600, a charter to the "Governor and Company of Merchants of London trading into the East Indies." This company was soon to rise to paramount power in the Indian sub-continent. *East India Company*

The chief commercial hopes of the new company, however, were not based on India. Rather it hoped to break into the rich trade of the East Indian spice islands. Spices were clearly the commodity to aim for. Since much of Europe's livestock had to be slaughtered before each winter, spices were needed to preserve meat during the cold season. Spices also flavoured food and hid the taste of bad meat. But the spice islands (small islands like Amboyna, Ternate and Tidore, as well as the large East Indian islands of Java, Sumatra, and the Celebes) already traded busily with the Dutch. Perhaps the English East India Company would not find it so easy to break in.

The first voyage Still, preparation went ahead for the first voyage. Among the two hundred or so subscribers to the company were these men (8):

Nicholas Barnsley, Grocer, £150
Henry Bridgman, Leatherseller, £200
James Deane, Draper, £300
Thomas Farrington, Vintner, £200
Leonard Halliday, Alderman, £1,000
Ralph Hamer, Merchant Tailor, £200
Sir Stephen Seame, Lord Mayor of London, £200
Thomas Smithe, Haberdasher, £200
Sir Richard Saltonstall and his children, £200
Richard Wiseman, Goldsmith, £200.

Five vessels commanded by James Lancaster set sail on 13th February, 1601. Among the goods they carried were: "40 muskets; 18 swords; a pair of bellows; a standing bed with pillows . . . and curtains; 3 old brass ladles; 26 sponges."

Sumatra Eighteen months later the expedition reached northern Sumatra. Here, the local ruler welcomed them as representatives of the power that had defeated the Spanish Armada in 1588. He granted them freedom to trade, and proceeded to question them: "The King asked our General if our Queen were married, and how long she reigned, which when the General had answered by his interpreter, the King wondered. The King likewise told the General, if the words in her Majesty's letter came from the heart, he had cause to think well thereof. Dinner being ended, the King caused his Damsels to dance, and his women to play Music unto them, who were richly adorned with Bracelets and Jewels, and this was a great favour: for he does not usually let them be seen to any (9)."

14 Although the Sumatrans had no use for many of the goods

brought by the English—woollen vests and Devon trousers, for example—this first contact of the East India Company with the Indies had been friendly enough. James Lancaster added profit to goodwill when he plundered a laden Portuguese galleon in the Indies before sailing for home.

Between 1601 and 1623 the English East India Company co-existed uneasily with the Dutch East India Company in the Indies. The Indonesians hated the Portuguese, and were glad to see them ousted by the two Protestant powers; but the Dutch were increasingly jealous of English activities. *Dutch competition*

The directors of the English East India Company were well aware of this: "If the present misunderstandings between the two nations should ferment to an open war, it would be thought by the vulgar but a war for pepper which they think to be [a] slight thing, because each family spends but a little [on] it. But at the bottom it will prove a war for the Dominion of the British as well as the Indian seas, because if ever they come to be sole masters of that Commodity, as they already are of nutmegs, mace, cloves, and cinnamon, the sole profit of that one commodity pepper being of general use, will be more to them, than all the rest and in probability sufficient to defray the constant charge of a great navy in Europe (10)."

In 1623 the Massacre of Amboyna, in the spice islands, snuffed out the hopes of the English in the East Indies. Nineteen Englishmen were arrested on a trumped-up charge of conspiracy by the Dutch Governor of Amboyna, Van Speult. Confessions were tortured out of the unlucky prisoners, ten of whom were executed. The violent reaction that these events provoked in England was not turned to good use. By 1682 the last English factory (or trading centre) in the spice islands had been abandoned. *Massacre of Amboyna*

Expelled from the East Indies the English now concentrated on India as a second-best. Fortunately the East India Company had made a landing on Indian soil in 1608. In that year William Hawkins arrived at Surat, a booming port on the west coast of India. The Portuguese were already established at Surat and did not welcome Hawkins. Indeed, he "could not peep out of doors for fear of the Portugals, who in troops lay lurking in *Portuguese competition*

Jahangir granted the East India Company the right to build this factory
at Surat in 1612

the by-ways to give me assault to murder me (11)." Nor did the
Portuguese think much of Hawkins' letter from King James I.
They "most vilely abused his Majesty, terming him King of
fishermen and of an island of no importance (12)."

Undeterred, Hawkins at last set off with a hired retinue for
Agra, the capital of the Mogul Emperor Jahangir (1605–28).
This expedition clearly shows the humble beginnings of the
English in India. Hawkins was just a lowly ambassador in a
sub-continent where great civilizations had once flourished,
and which teemed with millions of people, and with conflicting
religions and cultures.

Hawkins and Jahangir

The Mogul Emperor was of Turkish origin. He spoke
Persian and practised the faith of Islam, and ruled over a vast
number of subject territories. For the moment Mogul suzer-
ainty was effective, though its supremacy was soon to vanish.
Although the Moguls were Muslims, seventy per cent of the
Indian people were followers of the Hindu religion. Less than
ten per cent (like Buddhists, Sikhs or Parsees) avowed other

17

Opposite William Hawkins, a representative of the East India
Company, visited the court of the Mogul Emperor, Jahangir, at Agra
in 1608

faiths. Thus, with only twenty per cent of the Indian people belonging to Islam, the Mogul Emperors exercized a tactful sway in religious matters.

Emperor Jahangir welcomed Hawkins to his magnificent court. He was impressed by the Englishman's ability to speak Turkish and also by his drinking capacity! He made Hawkins a senior member of his staff and found him a Christian Armenian girl for a wife. Hawkins wrote to the East India Company that he hoped all this would "feather my nest and do you service (13)." The Company, however, got little out of it. Jahangir was not yet prepared to help the English at the expense of the Portuguese.

Roe's mission

In 1612 an English sea victory over the Portuguese, off Surat, persuaded Jahangir to grant the East India Company Surat as a factory. But this meant little more than the right to trade. The Portuguese were still dangerous rivals, and the favours of the Mogul Emperor could be withdrawn at any moment. In 1615, therefore, the East India Company sent Sir Thomas Roe on a well-provided mission to the Court of the Great Mogul in Agra.

Roe refused to admit any inferiority before Jahangir: "I passed on until I came to a place railed in right under him [Jahangir] with an ascent of three steps where I made him reverence and he bowed his body; and so went within it. I demanded a chair, but was answered no man ever sat in that place, but I was desired as a courtesy to ease myself against a pillar, covered with silver that held up his canopy (14)."

Surat: English base

Roe stayed at the Great Mogul's court for more than three years, trying to extract better trade terms for his Company, and also satisfying Jahangir's curiosity with this proud alien. Roe did not relish staying on at Agra, exclaiming, "I would sooner die than be subject to the slavery the Persian [ambassador] is content with (15)." At last, Roe did obtain permission for the Company to open factories in certain Indian towns. This really made Surat a permanent base for English trade, and possibly for expansion. Roe's proud and dignified conduct reflected well on his nation, which was then showing its naval strength to the Indians.

18   But Roe did not relish wars of conquest. He argued that the

Portuguese and the Dutch used up all their eastern profits in military adventures: "It is the beggaring of the Portugal, notwithstanding his many rich residences and territories, that he keeps soldiers that spend it, yet his garrisons are mean. He never profited by the Indies, since he defended them. Observe this well. It hath been also the error of the Dutch, who seek plantation here by the sword. They turn a wonderful stock, they prowl in all places, they possess some of the best; yet their dead pays consume all their gain. Let this be received as a rule that if you will profit, seek it at sea, and in quiet trade; for without controversy, it is an error to affect garrisons and land wars in India." Roe also claimed that "my sincerity toward you in all actions is without spot; my neglect of private gain is without example, and my frugality beyond your expectation (16)."

From 1619, when Roe left Agra, until 1640, Surat was the chief base of the English in the east. Then in 1640 Francis Day, a Company representative in southern India, obtained from a local Hindu raja a strip of land on which was built the fortified factory of St. George. From these humble beginnings grew the great bastion of British power in south east India—Madras. *Madras*

From the start of the English Civil Wars in 1642 to the Restoration of Charles II in 1660, the Company made no further startling advance. But in 1661 Charles II's bride, the Portuguese Princess Catherine of Braganza, brought Bombay as part of her dowry. By 1668 King Charles had rented Bombay, the finest port on the west Indian coast, to the Company. Interests on the Ganges delta led, by 1690, to the founding of the fortified factory of Fort St. William, around which grew the enormously successful but unhealthily situated city of Calcutta, in the densely populated province of Bengal. The basic pattern of the East India Company's land holdings was now clear. *An Indian dowry*

English activities in India caused much controversy and comment at home. Life for the Company's servants was often unpleasant and sometimes short. Englishmen in Surat or Madras or Calcutta continued to wear thick clothing, eat a heavy meal at midday, and drink too much wine. One Company *Dangers of trade*

A view of one of the Company's early fortified settlements at Calcutta

man complained that "at home men are famous for doing nothing; here they are infamous for their honest endeavours. At home is respect and reward; abroad is disrespect and heartbreaking. At home is augmentation of wages; abroad no more than the third of wages. At home is content; abroad nothing so much as grief, cares and displeasure. At home is safety; abroad no security. At home is liberty; abroad the best is bondage (17)."

In order to soften the Englishman's life in Bombay the East India Company sent out twenty single women of "sober and civil lives" in the early 1670s. But all did not go smoothly. The Company found that some of the women "are grown scandalous to our nation, religion and government", and the proper authorities were told to "give them all fair warning that they do apply themselves to a more sober and Christian conversation, otherwise the sentence is this, that they shall be confined totally of their liberty to go abroad, and fed with bread and

Bombay acquired a scandalous reputation in the 1670s when 20 women, sent out by the Company to brighten the lives of their representatives there, behaved badly and were threatened with deportation!

water till they are embarked on board ship for England (18)."

Bombay was not the only den of iniquity. In 1676 the Company's chaplain wrote a scandalized letter to the directors concerning the moral state of the English community in Madras: "I have the charity to believe that most of you have so much zeal for God, and for the credit of religion, that your heads would be fountains of water, and eyes rivers of tears, did you really know how much God is dishonoured, his name blasphemed . . . by the vicious lives of many of your servants . . .

Morals in Madras

"I do earnestly wish there may be more inspection taken what persons you send over into these places; for there come hither some thousand murderers, some men stealers, some popish, some come over under the notion of single persons and unmarried, who yet have their wives in England, and here have lived in adultery . . . Some on the other hand have come over as married [couples] of whom there are strange suspicions they were never married . . .

21

"Others pride themselves in making others drink till they be insensible, and then strip them naked, and in that posture cause them to be carried through the streets to their dwelling place. Some of them, with other persons whom they invited, once went abroad to a garden not far off, and there continued a whole day and night drinking most excessively, and in so much that one of the number died within a very few days after (19)."

Trading problems If the conduct of some of the Company's servants aroused debate, so did the matter of trade with India. English-made goods were not always easy to exchange for Indian merchandise. The Company had to plug the trade gap between imports and exports by paying for some Indian goods in silver bullion.

The economic and social problems raised by Indian trade were well expressed in the late 1600s by Henry Martyn: "There is no reason, that the Indians will take off any of our manufacturers, as long as there is such a difference in the price of English and Indian labour, as long as the labour or manufacture of the East Indies shall be valued there at but one-sixth part of the price of like labour or manufacture here in England ... Therefore, unless now and then for curiosities, English manufacturers will seldom go to India.

"Without the help of laws, we shall have little reason to expect any other returns for our bullion, than only manufactures, for these will be most profitable. For the freight of unwrought things from India is equal to the freight of so much manufacture; the freight of a pound of cotton is equal to so much callico; the freight of raw silk to that of wrought silk. But the labour by which this cotton or raw silk is to be wrought in England is a great deal dearer than the labour by which the same would be wrought in India.

"Therefore of all things which can be imported thence, manufactures are bought cheapest; they will be most demanded here, the chief returns will be on these. Little then will be returned from India besides manufactures. And when these shall be imported here they will be likely to stay. In France, Venice, and other countries, Indian manufactures are prohibited. The great consumption must be in England.

"It has been proved by arguments that bullion and chiefly

bullion is carried into India, that chiefly manufactures must be returned, and that these must be consumed in England. But instead of all other arguments, is matter of fact: cargoes of bullion are every year carried into India, while almost every one at home is seen in Indian manufactures . . .

"The next complaint against this trade is of the labourer: that he is driven from his employment to beg his bread; by the permission of Indian manufactures to come to England, English manufactures must be lost (20)."

Since the Company continued to diversify its trade in the East—beginning to trade in China tea in 1700 for example—the early problems of commerce with India were less painful than they might have been. The first century of the East India Company's history was thus one of fairly steady, if unspectacular, progress.

The political and military position of the Company, however, remained precarious. Portuguese and Dutch hostility was one thing; quite another was the disintegration of Mogul power which began later in the reign of the Emperor Aurangzeb (1658–1707). Shivaji, the great Maratha leader, began to assert his independence in west-central India. For a time the Maratha Confederacy was to achieve a paramount position in India. The prestige of Shivaji rivalled that of the Great Mogul himself, as can be seen in a description of the former's coronation in 1674: "The coverings of the royal seat were a grotesque combination of ancient Hindu asceticism and modern Mogul luxury: tiger skin below and velvet on top. On the two sides of the throne various emblems of royalty and government were hung from gilded lance-heads. On the right stood two large fish-heads of gold with very big teeth, and on the left several horses' tails (the insignia of royalty among the Turks) and a pair of gold scales, evenly balanced (the emblem of justice) on a very costly lance-head. All these were copied from the Mogul Court. At the palace gate were placed on either hand pitchers full of water covered with bunches of leaves, and also two young elephants and two beautiful horses, with gold bridles and rich trappings. These were auspicious tokens according to Hindu ideas (21)."

Decline of Moguls

23

*The ideal
Company man*

Not only was the Company's position at Surat, Bombay, and Madras threatened by the growing anarchy, but Calcutta was at risk, too. The directors of the Company were anxious to appoint men of high calibre in these testing times. When in 1687 they chose a new member of the Council for Madras (or Fort St. George) they insisted that he was "a man of learning, and competently well read in ancient histories of the Greeks and Latins, which with a good stock of natural parts only can render a man fit for government and political science, martial prudence and other requisites to rule over a great city . . .

"For its not being bred a boy in India, or staying long there and speaking the language or understanding critically the trade of the place, that is sufficient to fit a man for such a command as the Second of Fort St. George is, or may be, in time, though all these qualifications are very good in their kind (22)."

*Peace in
danger*

But good men could do little without proper support from home. Amid the decline of Mogul power, persuasive voices began to call for a policy of military consolidation in India. An Englishman called Job Charnock described the pitiful state of Bengal in 1678: "The whole Kingdom is lying in a very miserable feeble condition, the great ones plundering and robbing the feebler (23)."

Gerald Aungier, however, advocated a cure: "The state of India . . . is much altered of what it was; that justice and respect, wherewith strangers in general and especially those of our nation were wont to be treated with, is quite laid aside; the name of the honourable Company and the English nation through our long patient sufferings of wrong, is become slighted; our complaints, remonstrances, paper protests, and threatenings are laughed at . . .

"In violent distempers violent cures are only successful . . . the times now require you to manage your general commerce with your sword in your hands (24)." The sword was to play a larger part in furthering the fortunes of the East India Company.

Not all threats to the Company came, however, from India itself. After William of Orange came to the English throne in 1688, he allowed the formation of a New East India Company in 1698. Other traders were given a free hand in Indian commerce. The old and the new company competed briefly, and not very profitably, with each other. Finally, amalgamation seemed the only sensible solution. In 1708 the United Company of Merchants of England Trading to the East Indies was formed. This body was to last for almost 250 years, until the catastrophe of the Indian Mutiny of 1857.

The United Company (1698)

2 The Company Achieves Supremacy in India, 1708–1818

BY THE END of the Napoleonic War in 1815, the British East India Company had become the dominant power in India. The Company had contained, and eventually crushed, the challenge of the French East India Company. It had also pushed aside the Dutch and the Portuguese in the struggle for commercial mastery. By 1815, other European powers merely held small pieces of Indian territory: the Portuguese had Goa, Daman, and Diu; the French had Pondicherry, Mahe, Chandernagore, Yanaon and Karikal. These bases might have posed a military threat to the British, but the supremacy of the Royal Navy, and the general support of the home government, helped to ensure the eventual triumph of British interests.

Company power

During the eighteenth century Britain fought France three times for supremacy in India. The first struggle came during the War of the Austrian Succession (1740–48); the next was an unofficial war in India from 1750–54; the final and conclusive conflict came during the Seven Years' War (1756–63). The French were doing well until the early 1750s. The determined Governor of Pondicherry, Dupleix (Governor 1742–54), made a flying start in the struggle for power, and it was not until Robert Clive emerged as a soldier of genius that the balance tilted in favour of the British. Robert Clive, who was Governor of Bengal from 1757–60, and again from 1765–67, finally crushed the French and their Indian allies in that province at the great battle of Plassey in 1757.

England versus France

This victory brought the large and heavily populated province of Bengal under the rule of the East India Company.

27

Opposite Robert Clive was the architect of British supremacy in the sub-continent

The Nawab's artillery at the battle of Plassey. Clive won the battle against the French and their native allies and thus brought the vast province of Bengal under the rule of the East India Company

By 1818 the British had also defeated the Marathas and reduced the Mogul Emperor in Delhi to the status of a puppet ruler without power.

Maratha raids   It took three gruelling wars to break the Maratha Confederacy. But the Marathas had often made enemies among the Indian people by their raiding and looting, as described by a Bengali poet: "The *bargis* [horsemen] came up and encircled them [the fleeing villagers] in the plain. They snatched away gold and silver, rejecting all else. Of some people they cut off the hand, of some the nose and ears; some they killed outright. They dragged away the beautiful women, tying their fingers to their necks with ropes . . .

"After looting in the open, the *bargis* entered the villages. They set fire to the houses, large and small, temples and dwelling places. After burning the villages they roamed on all sides plundering. Some victims they tied with their arms twisted behind them. Some they flung down and kicked with their shoes. They constantly shouted, 'Give us rupees, give us rupees, give us rupees!' When they got no rupees, they filled their victims nostrils with water and drowned them in tanks. Some were put to death by suffocation. Those who had money gave it to the *bargis*; those who had none gave up their lives (25)."

The decline in the power of the Mogul Empire was com- *Mogul decline* pleted by the start of the nineteenth century. In the mid-eighteenth century the Frenchman Jean Law described Shah Alam who was crowned Emperor in 1759: "The *Shahzada* passed for one of those who have had the best education and who have most profited by it. This education consists particularly in the knowledge of religion; of the Oriental tongues, and of history, and in the writing of one's academic exercises well. In effect, all that I could perceive decided in his favour. He is familiar with the Arabic, Persian, Turki, and Hindustani languages. He loves reading and never passes a day without employing some hours in it ... He is of an enquiring mind, naturally gay and free in his private society, where he frequently admits his principal military officers in whom he has confidence (26)."

By 1803 Shah Alam, now an old man with his former glory stripped from him, saw the British march into Delhi: "At length the Commander-in-Chief was ushered into the royal presence, and found the unfortunate and venerable Emperor, oppressed by the accumulated calamities of old age, degraded authority, extreme poverty, and loss of sight, seated under a small tattered canopy, the remnant of his royal state, with every external appearance of the misery of his condition (27)."

Meanwhile, the British East India Company had been engaged in a crisis of conscience over its standards of administration. When faced with widespread bribery and corruption in India, the servants of the Company had frequently used the same methods in their dealings with Indians.

Warren Hastings' Governorship of Bengal (1772–85) had *Warren* brought these problems to a head. Hastings had been sent out *Hastings* 29

Shah Alam, one of the last great Mogul Emperors, sees the troops of the
British East India Company march into Delhi in 1803

to India to end corruption there; he had returned to face
charges that he had been guilty of the same thing. During his
time in India, Hastings had been constantly criticized by one
of his advisers, Philip Francis. In the end, Hastings fought a
duel with Francis, and beat him: "His pistol went off at the
same time, and so near the same instant that I am not certain
which was first, but believe mine was first and that his followed
in the instant. He staggered immediately, his face expressed a
sensation of being struck, and his limbs shortly but gradually
went under him, and he fell saying, but not loudly, 'I am dead.'

"I ran to him, shocked, I own, at the information . . . The
Seconds also ran to his assistance. I saw his coat pierced on the
right side, and feared the ball had passed through him; but he
sat up without much difficulty several times and once attempted

Warren Hastings, Governor of Bengal 1772–85, attempted to check widespread corruption in the Company's administration but was himself impeached before the House of Commons on his return to England

with our help to stand, but his limbs failed him and he sank to the ground. Colonel W. then proposed that as we had met from a point of honour and not for personal rancour, we should join hands . . . We did so, Mr. F. cheerfully; and I expressed my regret at the condition to which I saw him reduced (28)."

Warren Hastings sailed for home convinced that he had saved India for Britain. On board ship he wrote: "I have saved India, in spite of them all, from foreign conquest . . . [I have]

Hastings' diary

A cartoon by Gilray satirising the impeachment of Hastings. Burke (left) and Lord North (middle) led the attack on him in the House of Commons

become the instrument of raising the British name, and the substantial worth of its possessions in India, to a degree of prosperity proportioned to such a trust. [Yet both have vanished] in an instant, like the illusions of a dream, with the poor and only consolation left me of the conscious knowledge of what I could have effected, had my destiny ordained it (29)."

Impeachment of Warren Hastings

In 1788, three years after returning home, Hastings was impeached (that is, brought to trial) before the House of Lords. The great Parliamentarian, Edmund Burke, led the attack on him. The impeachment dragged on from 1788 to 1795. In the end, Hastings was acquitted of the charges brought against his administration in India. But his reputation and fortune had by now vanished. Only toward the end of his life was his work in India seen in its true light.

Regulating Act (1773)

The impeachment of Hastings can be seen as part of a larger, and more important, debate about the purpose of the Company's rule in India. Millions of non-European subjects had been acquired with the annexation of Bengal: should commercial interests dominate the Company's policymaking? Gradually the State came to play a larger part in the Company's affairs. Parliament passed the Regulating Act in 1773, which named a Governor-General for Bengal (and four advisers) who was able to supervise the Governors of Bombay and Madras.

The Regulating Act, however, was a rather feeble measure of intervention. In 1783 Charles James Fox, the Whig reformer, introduced his India Bill. Fox's Bill tried to give Parliament greater control over the administration in British India, while leaving commercial matters to the Company. After much political in-fighting, and the open hostility of King George III, the Bill was rejected in the House of Lords, and the Fox-North coalition government fell.

William Pitt the younger—son of the great Earl of Chatham —now emerged as Prime Minister. He presented his own India Bill in 1784. It became law the same year. It shared many of the features of Fox's India Bill. A Board of Control, responsible to Parliament, was set up. The Bill also gave Indian subjects of the Company equality before the law. Thus, not only had the State taken another large step toward control of administration in India, but it had asserted, indirectly perhaps, that Britain had a moral duty toward its Indian subjects. This "Dual Control" of Parliament and Company lasted until the Indian Mutiny of 1857.

The East India Company remained, of course, an enormously influential body, even though its trading activities by 1800 were less impressive than fifty years before. The vessels of "John Company" continued to plough a stately and generally comfortable passage, laden on the home trip with cargoes of tea, silks, chinaware and muslin. Captain Eastwick, a Company man, wrote: "These vessels were especially built for the service, and were generally run for about four voyages, when they were held to be worn out, and their places taken by others built for the purpose. About thirty ships were required for the company every year . . .

"The captain of an East Indiaman, in addition to his pay and allowances, had the right of free outward freight to the extent of fifty tons, being only debarred from exporting certain articles, such as woollens, metals, and warlike stores. On the homeward voyage he was allotted twenty tons of free freight, each of thirty-two feet; but this tonnage was bound to consist of certain scheduled goods, and duties were payable thereon to the company . . .

Company ships, or "East Indiamen", were specially built for the service.
Here they are engaging French war ships in action in 1804

"The gains to a prudent commander averaged from £4,000
to £5,000 a voyage, sometimes perhaps falling as low as
£2,000, but at others rising to £10,000 or £12,000. The time
occupied from the period of a ship commencing receipt of her
outward cargo to her being finally cleared of her homeward one
was generally from fourteen to eighteen months, and three or
four voyages assured any man a very handsome fortune (30)."

*Indian social
problems*
In India itself, officials and merchants grappled with problems of enormous complexity. Famine was an age-old curse,
and it struck Bengal hard in 1769–70: "The husbandmen sold
their cattle; they sold their implements of agriculture; they
devoured their seed grain; they sold their sons and their
daughters, till at length no buyer of children could be found;
they ate the leaves of trees and the grass of the field; and in
June 1770 the Resident at the Durbar affirmed that the living
were feeding on the dead.

"Day and night a torrent of famished and disease-stricken wretches poured into the great cities. At an early period of the year pestilence had broken out. In March we find smallpox at Moorshedabad, where it glided through the Viceregal mutes and cut off the Prince Syfut in his palace. Interment could not do its work quick enough, even the dogs and jackals, the public scavengers of the East, became unable to accomplish their revolting work, and the multitude of mangled and festering corpses at length threatened the existence of the citizens (31)."

Slavery still went on, despite Lord Cornwallis's attack on it in 1789, during his Governor-Generalship: "Hardly a man or woman exists in a corner of this populous town who hath not at least one slave child, either purchased at a trifling price or saved for a life that seldom fails of being miserable. Many of you, I presume, have seen large boats filled with such children coming down the river for open sale at Calcutta. Nor can you be ignorant that most of them were stolen from their parents or bought for perhaps a measure of rice, in time of scarcity (32)." *Slavery*

Indian society with its extremes of fabulous wealth and unspeakable poverty, with the rigid caste system of the Hindu religion, invited varied reactions from British observers. On the one hand there were those like the administrator Charles Grant who wrote: "We cannot avoid recognizing in the people of Hindostan a race of men lamentably degenerate and base; retaining but a feeble sense of moral obligation; yet obstinate in their disregard of what they know to be right, governed by malevolent and licentious passions, strongly exemplifying the effects produced on society by a great and general corruption of manners (33)."

James Mill, the British philosopher, dismissed Indian law as "a disorderly compilation of loose, vague, stupid or unintelligible quotations and maxims selected arbitrarily from books of law, books of devotion, and books of poetry; attended with a commentary which only adds to the absurdity and darkness; a farrago by which nothing is defined, nothing established (34)."

These low opinions of the Indian people had found popular justification in the infamous incident of the "Black Hole of *Black Hole of Calcutta*

Calcutta". During the Seven Years' War (1756–63) forces under the Bengali ruler Siraj-ad-daula captured Calcutta. Some 140 Britons were locked up in grossly cramped conditions. In the morning, 123 of them had died of suffocation. A contemporary account tells what happened, though perhaps in over-dramatic terms: "Observing every one giving way to the violence of passions, which I foresaw must be fatal to them, I requested silence might be preserved, whilst I spoke to them, and in the most pathetic and moving terms . . . I begg'd and intreated, that as they had paid a ready obedience to me in the day, they would now for their own sakes and the sakes of those who were dear to them, and were interested in the preservation of their lives, regard the advice I had to give them.

"I assured them, the return of day would give us air and liberty; urged to them, that the only chance we had left for sustaining this misfortune, and surviving the night, was the preserving a calm mind and quiet resignation to our fate. [I intreated] them to curb, as much as possible, every agitation of mind and body, as raving and giving a loose to their passions could answer no purpose, but that of hastening their destruction . . . Various expedients were thought of to give more room and air. To obtain the former, it was moved to put off their clothes. This was approved as a happy motion, and in a few minutes I believe every man was stripped.

"For a little time they flattered themselves with having gained a mighty advantage. Every hat was put in motion to produce a circulation of air, and Mr. Baillie proposed that every man should sit down on his hams. As they were truly in the situation of drowning wretches, no wonder they caught at every thing that bore a flattering appearance of saving them. This expedient was several times put in practice, and at each time many of the poor creatures whose natural strength was less than others, or had been more exhausted and could not immediately recover their legs, as others did when the word was given to rise, fell to rise no more. For they were instantly trod to death or suffocated.

"When the whole body sat down, they were so closely wedged together that they were obliged to use many efforts before they could put themselves in motion to get up again. Before nine o'clock every man's thirst grew intolerable (35)."

This disaster probably owed more to Indian carelessness than to cruelty and malice, but it lived on in British history as an example of barbarism. The reforming work of British missionaries, and the sympathetic attitudes of British administrators, may have had far less impact on the imagination of the average Briton. But just as there were those who criticized Indian society, there were those who believed that the beliefs and customs of that society should, in general, be respected.

The life of the British administrator in the Company's service was often hard and monotonous, despite the financial rewards. Marquis Wellesley, Governor-General from 1798–1805, described his lonely life: "Without my wife, I fear, I shall not have fortitude to remain here long enough to accomplish all my grand financial, military, naval, commercial, architectural, judicial, political reforms, and to make up a large treasure . . . All this might be effected within five or six years from the day of my embarkation at Cowes. But I leave you to judge of the necessity of her society while I give you some idea of my private life.

Wellesley in India

"I rise early and go out before breakfast, which is always over between eight and nine. From that hour until four, in the hot weather, I remain at work, unless I go to the Council, or to church on Sundays. At five I dine, and drive out in the evening. No constitution here can bear the sun in the middle of the day at any season of the year, nor the labour of the business in the evening. After dinner, therefore, nobody attempts to write or read, and, in general, it is thought necessary to avoid even meetings on subjects of business at that time; for in this climate good or ill health depends upon a minute attention to circumstances apparently the most trivial. Thus, in the evening I have no alternative but the society of my subjects, or solitude. The former is so vulgar, ignorant, rude, familiar, and stupid as to be disgusting and intolerable; especially the ladies, not one of whom, by-the-bye, is even decently good-looking.

"The greatest inconvenience, however, arises from the ill-bred familiarity of the general manners . . . The effect of this

The life of British administrators in Company service could be hard—
the climate took a heavy toll of health and spirits—but the compensations
included plentiful leisure and numerous servants

state of things on my conduct has been to compel me to entrench myself within forms and ceremonies, to introduce much state into the whole appearance of my establishments and household, to expel all approaches to familiarity, and to exercize my authority with a degree of vigour and strictness nearly amounting to severity . . .

Cornwallis in
India

"It required some unpleasant efforts to place matters on this footing, and you must perceive that I am forced to fly to solitude for a large portion of the twenty-four hours, lest I should weaken my means of performing my public duty (36)."

Lord Cornwallis, Governor-General from 1786 to 1793, was also under no illusions over his working day: "I get on horseback just as the dawn of day begins to appear, ride on the same road and the same distance, pass the whole forenoon after my return from riding in doing business, and almost exactly the same portion of time every day at table, drive out in a phaeton [light four-wheeled carriage] a little before sunset, then write or read over letters or papers on business for two hours; sit down at nine with two or three officers of my family to some fruit and a biscuit and go to bed soon after the clock strikes ten. I don't think that the greatest sap (swot) at Eton can lead a duller life than this (37)."

The minor servants of the Company found ways of breaking the boredom. Heavy drinking was one way, but insubordinate behaviour and gambling were also common. In 1711 the junior Company men at Fort St. George at Madras were the subject of concern: "We are sorry to hear that of late there has not been a sufficient decorum kept up among our people, and particularly among the young writers and factors, that there have been files of musketeers sent for to keep the peace at dinner time. . . . We direct that you the President and Council, do at certain stated seasons set apart a time to enquire into the behaviour of all our factors and writers . . . and calling them severally before you, let them know the account you have of them, and as they deserve either admonish or command them . . . It lies very much in your power to form their minds to virtue (38)." *Poor administration*

Drinking at the settlement of Bencoolen in Sumatra was the occasion for another firm dispatch in 1717 from the Company's Directors: "Could we once hear sobriety was become as fashionable on the West Coast as hard drinking hath been, we should entertain strong hopes that your new settlement at Marlborough . . . would give a better reputation to the West Coast than it hath hitherto had on account of health . . . it is positively affirmed you have good water, if you will be at the pains of fetching what is so. It is further said that a little tea boiled in the water doth admirably correct it, and that water kept till cold and so drank as water would contribute to the health of those who used it (39)."

By 1721 the directors were expressing their anxiety over gambling at Fort St. George: "It is with great concern we hear the itch of gaming hath spread itself over Madras, that even the gentle-women play for great sums, and that Capt. Seaton makes a trade of it to the stripping several of the young men there. We earnestly recommend to you to check as far as you can that mischevious evil. Let Capt. Seaton know if he continues that vicious practice he shall not stay but be removed, and do you take care he be sent off the shore. . . . And civilly acquaint the gentle-women that we desire they will put a stop to all high gaming, because first or last it will be prejudicial and ruinous to them or theirs (40)."

These earnest exhortations could not, of course, have much effect on bored roisterers half the world away. But the Company also had sober advice for those who bore the growing burden of administration in the eighteenth century. Dispatches to Bengal and St. Helena sent in 1714 and in 1717 set a tone which would not have been out of place in the high noon of the Victorian Raj: "We have always recommended to you to see justice administered impartially to all and speedily, to govern mildly and yet preserve authority. We have reason to add it here again for your remembrance, and earnestly to desire you will take care none under you be suffered to insult the natives, and that no voice of oppression be heard in your streets, this is the best method to enlarge our towns and increase our revenues (41)."

And later: "Never do an act of arbitrary power to hurt anybody. Let your determinations be always just, not rigorous but inclining to the merciful side. Always try the cause, never the Party. Don't let passion overcloud your reason. This will make the people respect you whereas one violent sentence or action will sully the reputation of ten good ones (42)."

These were not easy standards to live up to in the eighteenth century.

3 Towards the Abyss: The East India Company 1818–57

THE ENDING of the Third Maratha War in 1818 did not bring universal peace to India. The territory of the East India Company was steadily extended. These annexations were not always the result of long-term planning by the British. Rather local circumstances, and the need to hold and consolidate existing territory, encouraged a "forward" policy of expansion.

Military conquest

But even if the Company was slow to enter some of its wars of conquest, the final tally of military operations between 1818 and 1857 is impressive: 1824–26 First Burma War; 1839–42 First Afghan War; 1843 Sind conquered; 1844 defeat of province of Gwalior; 1845–46 First Sikh War; 1848–49 Second Sikh War (Punjab annexed); 1852 Second Burma War. In addition Nagpur was annexed in 1853, and Oudh in 1856. Other minor provinces were also brought under the Company's rule. By 1857 almost two thirds of the subcontinent had fallen to the British; the remaining states—ruled by various Indian princes—enjoyed a theoretical autonomy, but were in fact dominated by Britain.

Apart from the disastrous invasion of Afghanistan in 1839, the campaigns of the East India Company's armies had been triumphant. Some had even given rise to poetry in the stolid and Victorian-heroic mould:

THE FIELD OF FEROZSHAH
(First Sikh War, 1845)

Our wounded lay upon the ground,
But little help was nigh;
No lint or bandage for the wound!

41

They laid them down to die.
Their wounds unstaunch'd, with cold and thirst
Our heroes suffered then the worst
Upon that fatal plain.
Many a man whose wounds were slight
Thro' the fell horrors of that night
Will never fight again . . .

At length our gallant cavalry
Scarce fifteen hundred men,
The flower of Britain's chivalry
Prepare to charge again.
That gallant chieftain Colonel White,
These heroes bravely led;
They sought the hottest of the fight,
Their path was strewn with dead.
'Twas plainly marked for all to see
Where charged our British cavalry.

By a young soldier (Sergeant Bingham)
who fought in that glorious campaign
(London, 1848).

But how were these newly acquired subjects to be treated—
Baluchis, Sikhs, Punjabis and the rest? One could admire the
military prowess of the north-west frontier tribes, and the stoic
and passive qualities of village India. But there were less
obedient subjects in the making in the great towns and cities.
The newly educated Indians might be especially troublesome
if they found British rule distasteful. In the early nineteenth
century, however, these problems were a long way off.

Subject
peoples
Social contacts between British and Indians lessened in the
nineteenth century. Indian aristocrats, of course, were still
quite acceptable to the British both as hosts and guests. Early
in the century, the Mogul court and the leading lights of
British society in Old Delhi mixed at official afternoon recep-
tions. An Englishwoman described the Indian guests: "A
perfect bevy of princes, suave, watchful, ready at the slightest
encouragement to crowd round the Resident, or the Com-
missioner, or the Brigadier, with noiseless white-stockinged
42　　feet. Equally ready to relapse into indifference when unnoticed.

Social contacts between the British and their Indian subjects were limited
but the Indian aristocracy and the Mogul Court were patronized

"Here was Mirza Mughal, the king's eldest son, and his two
supporters, all with lynx eyes for a sign, a hint, of favour or
disfavour. And here—a sulky sickly looking lad of eighteen—
was [Jivan Bakht, the queen's] darling, dressed gorgeously and
blazing with jewels which left no doubt as to who would be the
heir-apparent if she had her way. Prince (Abu Bakr) however,
scented, effeminate, watched the proceedings with bright eyes;
giving the ladies unabashed admiration and after a time
actually strolling away to listen to the music. Finally however,
drifting to the stables to gamble with the grooms over a quail
fight.

"Then there were lesser lights. [Ahsanullah Khan] the
physician, his lean plausible face and thin white beard suiting

his black gown and skull-cap, discussed the system of Greek medicine with the Scotch surgeon, whose fluent, trenchant Hindustani had an Aberdonian twang . . . A few rich bankers curiously obsequious to the youngest ensign, and one or two pensioners owing their invitations to loyal service made up the company (43)."

In Cawnpore, in the province of Oudh, the Nana Sahib entertained generously, dispensing pork (a meat forbidden to Muslims), and displaying European gadgets and wares that caused some amusement among his British guests. The latter "sat down to a table twenty foot long (it had originally been the mess table of a cavalry regiment), which was covered with a damask table-cloth of European manufacture, but instead of a dinner napkin there was a bedroom towel. The soup . . . was served up in a trifle-dish which had formed part of a dessert service belonging to the 9th Lancers—at all events, the arms of that regiment were upon it; but the plate into which I ladled it with a broken teacup was of the old willow pattern. The pilao [rice dish] which followed the soup was served upon a huge plated dish, but the plate from which I ate was of the very commonest description. The knife was a bone-handled affair; the spoon and the fork were of silver, and of Calcutta make. The plated side-dishes, containing vegetables, were odd ones; one was round, the other oval.

"The pudding was brought in upon a soup-plate of blue and gold pattern, and the cheese was placed before me on a glass dish belonging to a dessert service. The cool claret I drank out of a richly-cut champagne glass, and the beer out of an American tumbler, of the very worst quality (44)."

The number of Indian rajahs and maharajahs, however, was limited. As more British women came out to join their menfolk, the British communities in India became more and more self-sufficient, more sealed off from non-European society. In the seventeenth and eighteenth centuries British men had often married, or at least lived with, Indian women. This practice, which had produced quite large numbers of children of mixed blood, declined in the nineteenth century.

In remoter areas, though, it still happened, and was criti-

Opposite Lord Canning, the first Viceroy of India, decorating Indian princes who had remained loyal to the British during the Mutiny

cized: "When a man in office is under the power of a native woman, she invariably takes bribes, and he gets the credit for doing so; for she of course gives out that the Sahib shares in her extortions . . . Now, putting the principles of morality out of the question, it is evident that an officer who thus places himself into the hands of a Heathen woman, is wholly unfit for any situation of authority (45)."

British women in India became notorious for their gossip. *High society* The passing on of juicy bits of scandal became a pastime for many—almost an art: "In other parts of the world they talk about things, here they talk about people. The conversation is all personal, and, as such, you may be sure tolerably abusive. What did they find to say about one another? The veriest trifles in the world. Nothing is so insignificant as the staple of Calcutta conversation. What Mr. This said to Miss That, and what Miss That did to Mr. This. And then all the interminable gossip about marriages and no-marriages, and will-be marriages and ought-to-be marriages, and gentlemen's attention and ladies' flirtings, dress, reunions, and the last burrakhana [big dinner] (46)."

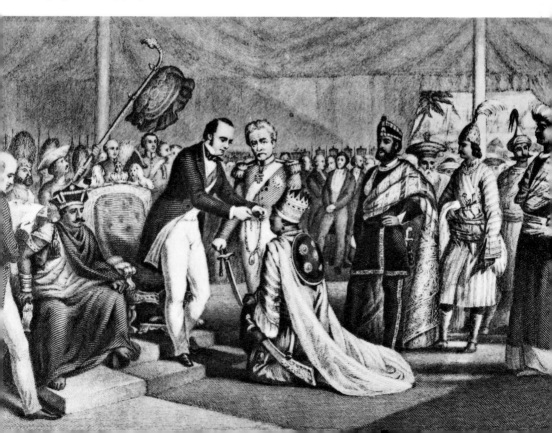

Or again: "'Mr. Collingwood,' returned Mrs. Parkinson, 'it really is quite shocking. He dined with us the day before yesterday—cholera, I suppose—dreadful!' and Mrs. Parkinson endeavoured to look quite overcome, but was not particularly successful. But Mrs. Poggleton pretended nothing at all: she leant forward, held out her hand for the undertaker's circular, looked rather pleased than otherwise, and said, 'Dear me! If it is not the gentleman with that pretty carriage, I declare!' 'Small use to him a pretty carriage now,' said Mrs. Parkinson, 'the only carriage that he needs is a hearse.' 'Oh; but', exclaimed Mrs. Poggleton, with more eagerness than she had manifested throughout the conversation, 'I have been dying a long time for that carriage, and now I shall be able to get it. What a nice thing to be sure!'

"Upon this Mrs. Parkinson lifted up her hands, and pretended to be immeasurably shocked, muttering to herself, but quite loud enough for everybody to hear, that life was a span, and death hanging over us, and that the world might be destroyed tomorrow, for anything she knew to the contrary, with sundry other moral reflections of this kind, equally original, and expressive of virtuous emotion (47)."

Indian service The main reason why so much gossiping took place was that women, even the wives of common soldiers, had time on their hands. This was not always an advantage, for it was "only just to notice the temptations, restraints, and miseries, to which this class of women are subject, in a country so little calculated to cherish their better feelings, or to provide them with necessary occupation, or common comfort. Unable, from extreme heat, to move out of the little room allotted to them in the 'married men's quarters', during the day, and provided, for two rupees a month, with a Portuguese 'cook boy', who relieves them from the toil of domestic duties, the only resource of the soldiers' wives is in mischievous associations, discontented murmurings, and habits of dissipated indulgence. Strolling in the evenings through the dirty bazaars of a native town, probably under the auspices of an ayah (Indian nurse) who may have picked up a smattering of the English language, these unhappy women purchase liquor, to conciliate their careless

The wives of British officials in nineteenth century India could lead lives of almost total indolence—the numbers of servants meant that they literally need do nothing for themselves

husbands. On returning late to the barracks, the truant wife frequently finds her partner already in a state of intoxication. Mutual recrimination follows, and then succeeds a scene for which we may well weep, that humanity has such (48)."

For the better-off families, servants were plentiful and cheap. They were not always treated very well. They were "often visited with blows and such abuse as no respectable man will bear; very often too for no other fault than that of not understanding what the master has said, who has given his directions in some unintelligible stuff from ignorance of the language, that no one could understand (49)."

Kindness was not always understood by servants: "One day I said to my ayah (a very elegant lady in white muslin), 'Ayah, bring me a glass of toast-and-water if you please.' She crept to the door and then came back again, looking extremely per-

Society gossip

47

plexed, and whined out, 'What Mistress tell? I don't know.' 'I told you to bring me some toast-and-water.' 'Toast-water I know very well, but Mistress tell if you please; I don't know if you please' (50)."

If British women were busy with the rather inward-looking world of the European community, with servant problems, and bringing up small children in a difficult climate, their menfolk got on with the task of governing the Company's possessions. As commerce became a smaller part of the Company's activities, the administration and the army provided the twin pillars on which British interests rested.

Recruits into the civil service had to pass a fairly stiff entrance examination into the Company's college at Haileybury: "Each candidate shall be examined in the four gospels of the Greek Testament, and shall not be deemed duly qualified for admission to Haileybury College, unless he be found to possess a competent knowledge thereof. *Joining the service*

"Nor unless he be able to render into English some portion of the works of one of the following Greek authors: Homer, Herodotus, Xenophon, Thucydides, Sophocles, and Euripides.

"Nor unless he can render into English some portion of the works of one of the following Latin authors: Livy, Terence, Cicero, Tacitus, Virgil, and Horace; and this part of the examination will include questions in ancient history, geography, and philosophy.

"Each candidate shall also be examined in modern history and geography, and in the elements of mathematical science, including the common rules of arithmetic, vulgar and decimal fractions, and the first four books of Euclid. He shall also be examined in moral philosophy, and in the evidences of the Christian religion as set forth in the works of Paley (51)."

If he passed through Haileybury, the new recruit sailed at his own expense round the Cape of Good Hope to one of the three "presidencies"—Bengal, Madras or Bombay. The price of a cabin out could be £100, without any furniture! The voyage was a tedious one and lasted between three and four months. At least it got the new man used to heat and boredom.

Recruits to the Company's army passed through the military *Indian army*

Opposite British wives did not even need to care for their own children; they could entrust them to an Indian *Ayah*, or nursemaid

college at Addiscombe, before sailing for India. The army in India numbered some 200,000, the vast majority of whom were sepoys (Indian troops); there were perhaps 5,000 British officers. The company's officers were often sought after as social lions: "In Europe there are separate classes of people who subsist by catering for the amusements of the higher classes of society, in theatres, operas, concerts, balls, etc., etc. But in India this duty devolves entirely upon the young civil and military officers of the government, and at large stations it really is a very laborious one, which often takes up the whole of a young man's time. The ladies must have amusement; and the officers must find it for them, because there are no other persons to undertake the arduous duty. The consequence is that they often become entirely alienated from their men, and betray signs of the greatest impatience while they listen to the necessary reports of their native officers, as they come on or go off duty (52)."

Even military duties were scarcely exhausting: "Well, a black rascal makes an oration by my bed every morning about half an hour before daylight. I wake, and see him salaaming (bowing) with a cup of hot coffee in his hand. I sit on a chair and wash the teaspoon till the spoon is hot and the fluid cold, while he introduces me gradually into an ambush of pantaloons and wellingtons—if there is a parade. I am shut up in a red coat, and a glazed lid set upon my head, and thus, carefully packed, exhibit my reluctance to do what I am going to do—to wit, my duty—by riding a couple of hundred yards to the parade (53)."

Barrack life   For other ranks, the barracks in India were as cheerless, noisy and rough as any back in Britain: "The barracks were exceptionally noisy. The passage was sounding and reverberating, and each occupant of a quarter had much of the benefit of his neighbour's flute, fiddle or French horn, whether 'i' the vein' for harmony or not; shoe brushings, occasional yells of servants undergoing the discipline of fists or cane, jolly ensigns and cadets clattering up and down, cracking horsewhips [and] whistling . . . On the ground might be seen a goodly display of trays, with egg shells, fish bones, rice, muffin, and other wrecks

Opposite Soldiers of the Bengal Infantry. The Company's Army was made up of about 5,000 British troops and the rest were Indian sepoys, or foot soldiers

A *nautsch*—a musical entertainment provided for the British authority
in Bengal in the 1830s

of breakfast; sweepers—certain degraded menials . . . squatting
near and waiting for the said remnants; hookahs . . . in course
of preparation for those who indulged in the luxury of
smoking (54)."

Looking back on his early Indian service, after a distinguished
career in the forces of the Empire, Lord Roberts wrote in 1898:
"The men were crowded into small badly-ventilated buildings,
and the sanitary arrangements were as deplorable as the state
of the water supply. The only efficient scavengers were the huge
birds of prey called adjutants, and so great was the dependence
placed upon the exertions of these unclean creatures that the
young cadets were warned that any injury done to them
would be treated as gross misconduct (55)."

Yet it was these poorly paid and harshly disciplined men who
carried the power of the East India Company into the remote
corners of the sub-continent. What was it all for? Military

Racing, together with polo—which was invented in India—were very popular sports with the British

glory? National prestige? Commercial advantage? Philanthropy? Improving the lot of the Indian people?

One British memsahib said of the Indians: "Thank goodness, I know nothing at all about them, nor I don't wish to. Really, I think the less one sees and knows of them the better (56)." This was hardly a benevolent attitude. Others saw the British role in India with more humility: "The most important of the lessons we can derive from past experience is to be slow and cautious in every procedure which has a tendency to collision with the habits and prejudices of our native subjects. We may be compelled by the character of our government to frame some institutions, different from those we found established, but we should adopt all we can of the latter into our system ... Our internal government ... should be administered on a principle of humility, not pride. We must divest our minds of all arrogant pretensions arising from the presumed superiority

The purpose of rule

53

The Barracks at Meerut, 1857. Barrack life could be cramped and insanitary and army pay was poor, but India was the goal of the dreams and aspirations of many young men in Victorian England

of our own knowledge, and seek the accomplishment of the great ends we have in view by the means which are best suited to the peculiar nature of the objects . . .

"All that Government can do is, by maintaining the internal peace of the country, and by adapting its principles to the various feelings, habits, and character of its inhabitants, to give time for the slow and silent operation of the desired improvement, with a constant impression that every attempt to accelerate this end will be attended with the danger of its defeat (57)."

Education in India   Unfortunately, the period from 1818 to 1857 saw increasing conflict between the Company and various sections of Indian society. Even attempts at educational reform antagonised some of those who were supposed to benefit. Thomas Macaulay, the historian, was a member of the Governor-General's Council in the early 1830s. In 1835 Macaulay argued as follows in a famous government minute: "To sum up what I have said: I think it is clear that we are free to employ our funds as we choose; that we ought to employ them in teaching what is best worth knowing; that English is better worth knowing than Sanskrit or Arabic; that the natives are desirous to be taught English, and are not desirous to be taught Sanskrit or Arabic; that neither as the languages of law, nor as the languages of religion, have the Sanskrit and Arabic any peculiar claim to our encouragement; that it is possible to make natives of this country thoroughly good English scholars, and that to this end our efforts ought to be directed.

"In one point I fully agree with the gentlemen to whose general views I am opposed. I feel, with them, that it is impossible for us, with our limited means, to attempt to educate the body of the people. We must at present do our best to form a class who may be interpreters between us and the millions whom we govern; a class of persons, Indian in blood and colour, but English in taste, in opinions, in morals, and in intellect. To that class we may leave it to refine the vernacular dialects of the country, to enrich those dialects with terms of science borrowed from the Western nomenclature, and to render them by degrees fit vehicles for conveying knowledge to the great mass of the population (58)."

Many Indians took advantage of the new European education thus offered, but others believed that the British were merely trying to train non-European servants of the East India Company. "The British Government," argued one Indian critic, "professes to educate the Natives to an equality with Europeans, an object worthy of the age and of Britain.

"But if Englishmen, after educating the Natives to be their equals, continue to treat them as their inferiors—if they deny the stimulus to honourable ambition, and show the Natives that there is a barrier over which superior Native merit and ambition can never hope to pass . . . are they not in effect undoing all that they have done, unteaching the Native all that he has been taught, and pursuing a suicidal policy, which will inevitably array all the talent, honour and intelligence of the country ultimately in irreconcilable hostility to the ruling power (59)?"

Suttee, the custom decreeing that a Hindu widow should be burnt alive
on her husband's funeral pyre, was abolished by the British in 1829

The education issue, however, did not affect many Indians.
The work of missionaries and evangelical Christians, which
was encouraged in the early 1800s, aroused much more
hostility. It seemed as though the British were attacking the
ancient religions of India. The Company also came down hard
on Indian customs that it considered uncivilized.

Widows burned alive

In 1829 the practice of *suttee* was declared illegal in Bengal,
an example later followed in other British provinces. *Suttee* was
the supposedly voluntary burning alive of Hindu widows on
the funeral pyres of their dead husbands. In 1818 a police
superintendent in lower Bengal wrote: "There are very many
reasons for thinking that such an event as a voluntary *suttee*
rarely occurs. Few widows would think of sacrificing themselves
unless overpowered by force or persuasion, very little of either
being sufficient to overcome the physical or mental powers of
the majority of Hindu females. A widow, who would turn with

natural instinctive horror from the first hint of sharing her husband's pile, will be at length gradually brought to pronounce a reluctant consent because, distracted with grief at the event, without one friend to advise or protect her, she is little prepared to oppose the surrounding crowd of hungry Brahmins and interested relations . . . In this state of confusion a few hours quickly pass, and the widow is burnt before she has had time to think of the subject.

"Should utter indifference for her husband, and superior sense, enable her to preserve her judgment, and to resist the arguments of those about her, it will avail her little. The people will not be disappointed of their show . . . The entire population of a village will turn out to assist in dragging her to the bank of the river, and in keeping her on the pile (60)."

Between 1829 and 1837 the Company also suppressed *thugee*. *The "thugs"* The "Thugs" were a band of robbers who strangled their victims as sacrifices to the goddess Kali. They were described as "the cunningest Robbers in the World. . . . They use a certain slip with a running noose which they can cast with so much slight about a Man's Neck when they are within reach of him, that they never fail; so that they strangle him in a trice (61)."

Female infanticide, the killing of unwanted girl babies, was *Unwanted* also commonplace. With so many mouths to feed poor families *girl babies* could not always afford to keep girl babies who would need dowries when they came to be married.

But this practice was not always just found in poor families. A landowner described how when his daughter "was born he was out in his fields . . . the females of the family put her into an earthen pot, buried her in the floor of the apartment where her mother lay, and lit a fire over the grave . . . He made all haste home as soon as he heard of the birth of a daughter, removed the fire and earth from the pot, and took out his child. She was still living, but two of her fingers which had not been sufficiently covered were a good deal burned. He had all possible care taken of her, and she still lives; and both he and his wife are very fond of her . . .

"He had given no orders to have her preserved, as his wife

was confined sooner than he expected. But the family took it for granted that she was to be destroyed . . . In running home to preserve her, he acted on the impulse of the moment. The practice of destroying female infants is so general among this tribe, that a family commonly destroys the daughter as soon as born, when the father is from home, and has given no special orders about it, taking it to be his wish as a matter of course (62)."

Indians defend traditions

The East India Company, which seemed conservative to the British, seemed radical and reforming to Indian traditionalists when it attacked practices like these. By the end of the Governor-Generalship of the energetic and confident Lord Dalhousie (1848–56) large sections of Indian opinion had been antagonised. Dalhousie's scheme to build a railway system aroused fears that the caste system would be damaged by the physical contact inevitable on crowded trains.

Annexation of Oudh

Moreover, Dalhousie had annexed several Indian provinces between 1848 and 1856. In 1856 he annexed Oudh, the last great independent Muslim state in North India. The pretext—internal disorder—was a reasonable one: "The landowners keep the country in a perpetual state of disturbance, and render life, property and industry everywhere insecure. Whenever they quarrel with each other, or with the local authorities of the Government, from whatever cause, they take to indiscriminate plunder and murder over all lands not held by men of the same class. No road, town, village or hamlet is secure from their merciless attacks. Robbery and murder become their diversion, their sport, and they think no more of taking the lives of men, women and children who never offended them than those of deer and wild hog. They not only rob and murder, but seize, confine, and torture all whom they seize and suppose to have money or credit till they ransom themselves with all they have or can beg or borrow (63)."

The resentments caused by the annexation of Oudh were to mingle with many other discontents. Within a year of Dalhousie's departure for Britain, and public acclaim, the great Mutiny threatened to sweep away the very foundations of British power.

4 The Great Mutiny, 1857–8

THE INDIAN MUTINY has been variously interpreted. To the Victorians it was simply a mutiny: a revolt by sepoys in the Army of Bengal. To some Indian nationalists it later became a freedom struggle, a war for Indian independence. The truth lies somewhere between these two extremes. There was a wide variety of causes: resentment at the westernising policies of the East India Company; fears for Indian religions; sympathy for thousands of landlords deprived of land to which they could not legally prove ownership; dislike of the superior attitudes of the British in India; hatred for the recent annexations during Lord Dalhousie's Governor-Generalship.

The spark that ignited the powder keg, however, was a military one. The new Enfield rifle was introduced into the East India Company's armies in 1857. To load the new weapon the sepoys had to bite open the end of a cartridge. The rumour went round that these cartridges were smeared with animal fat. Hindus considered the cow sacred; Muslims believed the pig to be unclean. Sepoys from both religious sects became convinced that the use of the Enfield rifle would be against their beliefs. The Company tried to stop trouble by withdrawing the offending cartridges, but they were too late.

Trouble with a rifle

At Meerut on 9th May, 1857, the whole garrison paraded to see eighty-five members of the 3rd Native Cavalry stripped of their medals and insignia, and marched off for ten years imprisonment for refusing to use the controversial cartridges. The divisional commander, Major-General ("Bloody Bill") Hewitt, had insisted on these retributions. The next day, the

Revolt at Meerut

59

three sepoy regiments at Meerut rose in rebellion, slaughtered their British officers, and set off for Delhi forty miles away.

Calcutta received the first news of the mutiny by a private telegram from Meerut: "The cavalry have risen setting fire to their own houses and several officers' houses, besides having killed and wounded all European officers and soldiers they could find near the lines. If aunt intends starting tomorrow evening please detain her from doing so as the van has been prevented from leaving the station (64)." Then there was silence. The telegraph line from Meerut had been cut.

The line from Delhi went dead next. The last message from there read: "The sepoys have come in from Meerut and are burning everything. Mr. Todd is dead and we hear several Europeans . . . We must shut up (65)."

The rebellion spread like a forest fire through Oudh—so recently annexed, and from where many of the sepoys in the Bengal Army were recruited. It also affected the north-east Rajput states and west Bengal. The centres of the Mutiny were Meerut, Delhi, Gwalior, Jhansi, Bareilly, Lucknow, Cawnpore, Allahabad and Benares. Although the sepoys led the way, large numbers of the civilian population supported them, or at least assumed that British rule had lapsed. *Sepoys up in arms*

But the mutineers had no coherent aims. Some wanted to restore the Mogul Emperor to his former glory; some wanted to reinstate the deposed King of Oudh. The only common factor was that they all wanted to restore some cherished piece of the past. In this sense, the Mutiny was a conservative reaction against the allegedly radical reforms of the East India Company, and in defence of the broad Indian tradition.

Compared with the Crimean War (1854–56) or the American Civil War (1861–65), the Indian Mutiny was a small-scale event. Only the Army of Bengal rose in rebellion. The armies of Madras and Bombay remained loyal. Newly conquered territories like the Punjab stayed quiet, and the Sikhs, indeed, helped to crush the revolt. The Indian princes, with few exceptions, did nothing to help the mutineers.

Yet the British were caught completely by surprise by the outbreak. The early months of the Mutiny belonged to the *British shock*

Opposite Bengal sepoys. The Indian troops at Meerut rebelled at having to bite off the ends of cartridges allegedly smeared with animal fat which offended their religious beliefs. This sparked off the Mutiny

British troops pushing forward to Delhi which was overrun by the
rebels at an early stage in the revolt

rebels. Only gradually did British reinforcements begin to
reconquer the trouble spots. Even then progress was slow.
Often, the sepoys fought to the last man rather than face the
terrible retribution that awaited them.

The Mutiny was rich in drama, and so full of horrors that the
Victorian imagination was stimulated for decades afterwards.
At Cawnpore the sepoys forced the surrender of the garrison in
three weeks. Several hundred British men, women and children
were massacred as they left Cawnpore under a supposed "safe
conduct":

MASSACRE AT CAWNPORE 1857

They ranged themselves to die, hand clasping hand—
That mournful brotherhood in death and woe—
While one with saddened voice, yet calm and slow,
Read holy words about yon better land,
Upon whose ever-blushing summer strand
Comes never shadow of a fiendish foe,
Nor hellish treachery like to that below
Is with malignant hatred coldly planned—

Then prayed. O Crucified, didst Thou not stoop
Down from above with Thy deep sympathy,
Soothing the suffering, bleeding, huddled group,
While the fierce vollies poured in hurriedly,
And with uplifted swords the yelling troop
Rushed to complete their deed of perfidy?

But all is over—the fierce agony
Of men who could not their beloveds save
From unheard tortures, and a common grave
Heaped high with quivering, crushed humanity—
The frantic woe of women forced to see
Their tiny infants, unto whom they clave
With love which could all fear and torment brave,
Dashed down upon the ground unpityingly:
And nought remains but the wet, bloody floor,
And little rings of soft, white baby-hair
Mingled with long, dark tresses, dimmed with gore,
In hopeless tangles scattered here and there,
And God's own blessed Book of holy lore,
Sole comforter amid that deep despair.

Mary E. Leslie, *Sorrows, Aspirations, and Legends
from India* (London, 1858)

Cawnpore had seen the storm clouds gathering early. Before
the siege a sepoy had told a British sergeant-major's wife in the
market-place: "You will none of you come here much oftener.
You will not be alive another week (66)." Nor was the defence
of Cawnpore impressive. One of Sir Henry Lawrence's aides
visited Lucknow before the siege and wrote that he had never
seen "so frightful a scene of confusion, fright and bad arrange-
ment as the European barrack painted. Four guns were in
position, loaded, with European artillerymen in night caps
and wide-awakes and side-arms on, hanging on to the guns in
groups—looking like melodramatic buccaneers. People . . . of
every colour, sect and profession were crowding into the
barracks . . . cargoes of writers, tradesmen . . . A miscellaneous
mob of every complexion from white to tawny, all in terror of
the imaginary foe. Ladies sitting down at the rough mess tables
in the barracks, women suckling infants, *ayahs* and children
in all directions. . . . If any insurrection took or takes place, we

63

The ruined residency at Lucknow riddled with bullet holes after the siege

shall have no one to thank but ourselves (67)."

Lucknow, in the province of Oudh, was also besieged. The garrison was commanded by the formidable Sir Henry Lawrence, who early on suffered a fatal wound. His nephew wrote: "About 8 o'clock, just before breakfast, when Uncle and I were lying in our beds, side by side, having just come in from our usual morning walk and inspection, and while Wilson, the Deputy Adjutant-General, was standing between our beds, reading some orders to Uncle, an eight-inch shell thrown from a howitzer came in at the wall, exactly in front of my bed, and at the same time burst. There was an instant darkness, and a kind of red glare, and for a second or two no one spoke. Finding myself uninjured, though covered with bricks from top to toe, I jumped up. At the same time Uncle cried out that he was killed. Assistance came, and we found that Sir Henry's left leg had been almost taken off, high up by the thigh (68)."

Lucknow soon suffered more horrors: "In a few minutes the cannonading and musketry fire were most terrific. We felt sure the enemy must get in, when the most terrible death awaited us. We sat trembling, hardly able to breathe, when Mrs. Case proposed reading the Litany . . . Poor Mrs. Palmer had her leg taken off by a round today, she, with some other ladies, having remained in the second storey of the Residency house . . .

"John said that he had made up his mind that every man should die at his post, but what were the sick and wounded, the women and helpless children, to do? The contemplation seemed too dreadful. At one time he talked of blowing us up at the last minute, but I have since heard this would have been impracticable. It was strange how calmly we talked on these subjects (69)."

The prospects facing the British families trapped in Lucknow were grim. At best they could hope that the siege would be short, and that food and drink would last out. At worst, they would have to face defeat and, very probably, savage death. The fate awaiting British women and children if the mutineers seized Lucknow was uncertain. There were fearful rumours of sepoy atrocities, of women raped, and babies tossed on bayonets for sport.

The residency at Lucknow with skeletons strewn on the ground in front

In Lucknow: "Several of the men contemplated the destruc- *Suicide pacts* tion of their females if the enemy should overpower us. I was, during those terrible days, one evening taken aside by a military man, who was one of my garrison. He had, he told me, agreed with his wife that if the enemy should force his way in, he should destroy her. She had expressed herself content to die by a pistol ball from his hand. He was, he told me, prepared, if I should fall, to do the same deed of despair to my own wife (70)."

Among the besieged were Katherine Bartrum, and her fifteen month-old son, Bobbie. Katherine had been sent into the Residency at Lucknow, unwillingly leaving her husband, Captain Robert Bartrum, at an out-station. A group of loyal sepoys escorted Katherine and her son into Lucknow. She did not trust them: "Sometimes they made our elephants stand whilst they lay upon the ground laughing and talking; but whenever I asked them for water for baby to drink, they would give it to me (71)."

Once safely inside the Residency of Lucknow, Katherine was "fully occupied in nursing, and washing our clothes, together with cups and saucers, and fanning away the flies which have become a fearful nuisance." When the children were asleep "we used to gather round a chair, which formed our tea-table, sitting on the bedside, and drinking our tea (not the strongest in the world) by the light of a candle which was stuck in a bottle . . . And then we talked together of bygone days, of happy homes in England where our childhood had been spent (72)."

The relief of Lucknow. The defenders held out against a terrible bombardment and after the commander, Sir Henry Lawrence, had been mortally wounded early in the siege

Eventually the forces of Generals Outram and Havelock fought their way into Lucknow. But they were not strong enough to break out again. Captain Bartrum was killed just as he was reaching the safety of the Residency. The widowed Katherine endured the double ordeal of grief, and a prolonged siege. She lacked soap, so "we have to use the *dhal* (peas) by grinding it between two stones and making it into flour, and this is a good substitute for soap. But we have so little of it, that it is a question sometimes whether we shall use it to wash with, or to eat (73)." *Reinforce-ments trapped*

When Katherine finally left Lucknow in November, 1857, she wrote: "Heard that we are to leave Lucknow tomorrow night, with just what we can carry. Well! I can only carry my baby, and my worldly effects can be put into a very small compass, since they consist merely of a few old clothes. My heart fails me at the thought of the terrible march, with no one to look after me or care for me but God. I have lost my kind friend Dr. Darby, who has been wounded; and they say he will not recover. He promised to take care of me on the journey to Calcutta, but now I am utterly friendless (74)."

She did reach Calcutta, but her child had been weakened by his deprivations; he sickened and died. Katherine sailed for England, widowed and childless. Her experiences were not unusual in the awful disruption caused by the Mutiny.

As the British troops fought their way into towns like Cawnpore, Lucknow and Delhi, they carried out terrible reprisals. The atrocities of the sepoys were repaid in kind. Mutineers were given, at best, short military trials. Mostly they were shot down, bayoneted, or hanged, sometimes in pigs' skins to defile Muslims, or in cows' skins to mortify Hindus. In many cases, mutinous sepoys were tied to the mouths of cannons and blown into fragments of flesh and intestine. *Bloody reprisals*

General Neill, in Cawnpore, enforced a punishment that was extraordinarily sadistic, even as revenge for the massacred women and children: "I wish to show the Natives of India that the punishment inflicted by us for such deeds will be the heaviest, the most revolting to their feelings and what they must ever remember ... The well (which had contained British *Neill's revenge*

69

Atrocities were committed by both sides in the Mutiny—and acts of heroism. The engraving shows Mrs Wheeler defending herself against the mutineers at Cawnpore

bodies) will be filled up, and neatly and decently covered over to form their grave . . . The house in which they were butchered, and which is stained with their blood, will not be washed or cleaned by their countrymen [but by] such of the miscreants as may hereafter be apprehended, who took an active part in the Mutiny, to be selected according to their rank, caste and degree of guilt. Each miscreant, after sentence of death is pronounced upon him, will be taken down to the house in question under a guard and will be forced into cleaning up a small portion of the blood-stains; the task will be made as revolting to his feelings as possible, and the Provost Marshal will use the lash in forcing anyone objecting to complete his task. After properly cleaning up his portion, the culprit is to be immediately hanged (75)."

The rebel town of Jhansi was ruthlessly sacked by the victorious British forces: "Fires were blazing everywhere, and although it was night I could see far enough. In the lanes and streets people were crying pitifully, hugging the corpses of their dear ones. Others were wandering, searching for food while the cattle were running mad with thirst . . . How cruel and ruthless were these white soldiers, I thought; they were killing people for crimes they had not committed . . . *Jhansi sacked*

"Not only did the English soldiers kill those who happened to come in their way, but they broke into houses and hunted out people hidden in barns, rafters and obscure, dark corners. They explored the inmost recesses of temples and filled them with dead bodies of priests and worshippers. They took the greatest toll in the weavers' locality, where they killed some women also. At the sight of white soldiers some people tried to hide in haystacks, in the courtyards, but the pitiless demons did not leave them alone there. They set the haystacks on fire and hundreds were burnt alive . . . If anybody jumped into a well the European soldiers hauled him out and then killed him, or they would shoot him through the head as soon as he bobbed out of the water for breath (76)."

The suppression of the Mutiny became a bloody assize, where the common British soldiers killed on the slightest suspicion: "I seed two Moors [Indians] talking in a cart. Presently I heard one of 'em say 'Cawnpore'. I knowed what that meant. So I fetched Tom Walker, and he heard 'em say 'Cawnpore', and he knowed what that meant. So we polished 'em both off (77)." *British terror tactics*

The London *Times* was soon growling that: "This blind and indiscriminate exasperation is resolving itself into the mere hatred of a dark skin." Generally, however, British opinion rejoiced in the overthrow of the mutineers. Citizens of good standing informed each other that: "The Sepoys have taken to inflicting the most exquisite cruelties upon the Sikhs, and the Sikhs in return swear that they will stamp the Company's arms in red-hot pice [copper coins] over the body of every Sepoy

71

Savage retribution was taken by the British once they gained the upper hand over the rebels

who comes in their way. These are the sort of tidings that nowadays fill every heart in England with exultation and thankfulness (78)."

"Clemency" Canning The Governor-General, Lord Canning (1856–62), found it very hard to restrain the orgy of revenge. But he succeeded, in part, in stemming the flood, and earned the nickname of "Clemency" Canning for his pains. Canning would not have liked the suggestion put forward in a Bombay newspaper that the whole city of Delhi be destroyed, and a plaque set upon a great pyramid to read (79):

BENEATH THIS PYRAMID
Lie Buried
A Palace, its King, its Princes
and the
Monsters of the Bengal Native Army they
Incited to Mutiny, to Murder, and Other
Crimes Unutterable.

Both sides fought with desperate ferocity—the sepoys had nothing to
lose and could expect no mercy if they failed; the British were fighting
for an Empire—and, as they thought, an ideal

STRANGER!
If you would know where
Delhi was,
Behold its Debris in the Pyramid
You Stand On
ANNO DOMINI MDCCCLVII

By the middle of 1858 the Mutiny had been crushed. The *The last of*
British swept away much of the old system of governing India. *the Moguls*
Among the first casualties of reform was the last Mogul
Emperor, Bahadur Shah II, who had been elevated by the
mutineers to a majesty more apparent than real. He was
described thus in captivity: "Sitting cross-legged on a cushion
placed on a common native *charpoy*, or bed, in the verandah
of a courtyard, was the last representative of the Great Mughal
Dynasty. There was nothing imposing in his appearance, save
a long white beard which reached to his girdle. About middle
height, and upwards of seventy years old, he was dressed in

73

white, with a conical-shaped turban of the same colour and material, while at his back two attendants stood, waving over his head large fans of peacocks' feathers, the emblem of sovereignty—a pitiable farce in the case of one who was already shorn of his regal attributes, a prisoner in the hands of his enemies. Not a word came from his lips. In silence he sat day and night, with his eyes cast on the ground (80)."

East India Company nationalized

If the Mogul Emperor had had his day, so had the Honourable East India Company. In November, 1858, a Royal Proclamation announced that: "Whereas, for divers weighty reasons, we have resolved, by and with the advice and consent of the Lords Spiritual and Temporal, and Commons, in Parliament assembled, to take upon ourselves the government of the territories in India, heretofore administered in trust for us by the Honourable East India Company (81)."

The British government took over the administration from the Company. The Governor-General assumed the title of Viceroy. In London, a Secretary of State for India was created with a seat in the Cabinet; he was given an India Council of fifteen members to advise him. Through the Secretary of State, Parliament was now directly responsible for British India. But Parliament tended to leave the day to day administration of India to the "men on the spot."

Army reforms

The Indian Army, naturally enough, was also reformed. The ratio of British to Indian troops was adjusted so that, ideally, Indians should never outnumber British by more than two to one. Indian troops were no longer allowed to handle artillery.

Conservatism wins the day

What were the other effects of the Great Mutiny? Certainly the British Raj became much more conservative, remembering how dangerous the pre-1857 reforms had proved. The British now tended to lean heavily for support on the more conservative elements in Indian society, such as the princes and landowners. But perhaps more important, the Mutiny further widened the social and cultural gap between the British and the Indians. Racial prejudice seemed justified in the terrible events of 1857–58. How, it was argued, could the British ever trust the treacherous Hindus and Muslims again? Some Indians, too, nursed bitter memories of British retribution.

74

5 *The Raj at its Height, 1858–1905*

THE HALF CENTURY after the Mutiny saw the British in India setting-up a complicated, but basically conservative, system of government. Now that the East India Company no longer ruled India, it was much easier to impose the ideas of the British government. The Indian Civil Service became an efficient, and on the whole very fair, means of administering India. At the top of the system was the Viceroy, who usually held office for four or five years. Under him there were the Governors of the different provinces like Madras, Bombay or the Punjab. Under the Governors were the civil servants, law officers, police chiefs and so forth.

After the Mutiny

The Viceroy could act the part of a reformer, or of a conservative, during his period of office. Between the Mutiny and 1905, it would be fair to say that only two Viceroys tried to introduce important new measures: Lord Ripon (1880–84), a Viceroy appointed by a Liberal government; and Lord Curzon (1898–1905), who was appointed by a Conservative government. Perhaps the main reason why few reforms were made during these years is that the British feared that they would build up resentments similar to those that had caused the Indian Mutiny.

The Viceroys

By the end of Queen Victoria's reign in 1901, the Viceroy was one of the most powerful rulers in the world, although he could, in theory, be recalled by the British government. He had some 300 million subjects. At his disposal was one of the finest armies in the world, the Indian Army. Both the Army and Indian Civil Service were paid for out of taxes gathered in India. In this way, the Indian people paid for the forces which

Landing goods at Calcutta in the 1860s. By the end of the nineteenth century India had become one of the most important commercial assets of the Victorian Empire

kept India part of the British Empire.

India was a very important part of the Victorian Empire—perhaps the most important part of all. Nineteen per cent of British exports went to India, and hundreds of millions of pounds sterling were invested there. Also, the Raj was thought to be a superb example of uncorruptible administration of a subject people by an imperial power. Thus for economic reasons, as well as for reasons of prestige, India was thought of as the "brightest jewel in the imperial crown".

In 1877 Queen Victoria was proclaimed Empress of India. This was the idea of the Conservative Prime Minister Benjamin Disraeli (1804–81). Disraeli believed that if his government gave Queen Victoria the new title it would make the Indian princes (who ruled one third of India) even more loyal in their support of the Raj. Queen Victoria never once visited India,

Victoria: Empress of India (1877)

77

Opposite Lord Curzon was one of the few late Victorian Viceroys who attempted to introduce reforms into the British administration of India

but she was proclaimed Empress with great pomp and ceremony.

The heads of the Indian Civil Service, the Indian princes, and thousands of troops attended the celebrations. The Indian princes brought their own troops and military bands: "One venerable gentleman ... had a man grinding *God save the Queen* on a hand organ, when we entered his tent. [Another] had a band of bagpipes, and gave us *God Bless the Prince of Wales*, played by pipers as black as soot, but with pink leggings on their knees to make them like their Highland originals (82)."

But when the new Empress was proclaimed, brass bands and trumpeters heralded the event as the Viceroy read out the proclamation. The massed infantry then fired their rifles in the air: "This was splendidly executed and with excellent effect, for it made the rajahs jump, and raised quite a stampede among the elephants, who 'skedaddled' in all directions, and killed a few natives (83)."

The Indian princes were given new coats-of-arms which were displayed on banners of heavy Chinese satin. The Viceroy, Lord Lytton (1876–80) wrote to Queen Victoria that the fault of the banners was "that the brass poles, which are elaborately worked, make them so heavy that it requires the united efforts of two stalwart Highlanders to carry one of them ... Consequently, the native chiefs who have received them will, in future processions, be obliged, I anticipate, to hoist them on the backs of elephants (84)."

Day-to-day rule The proclamation ceremony, however, was basically a spectacular episode amid the serious business of ruling a teeming and backward sub-continent. The everyday business of the Raj was to enforce law and order, to try to improve public health and public education, to advance irrigation schemes, and to deal with huge problems like famine control and agricultural efficiency.

The enormous size of these problems meant that progress was slow. It would have remained slow even if the Raj had spent money much more generously. Often the British administration played down the problems. Florence Nightingale (1820–1910), the famous nursing and medical reformer, surveyed health conditions in the Indian Army and wrote in 1863 that when

78

Opposite Queen Victoria was made Empress of India in 1877 at the instigation of Benjamin Disraeli, the Conservative Prime Minister

"NEW CROWNS FOR OLD ONES!"

(ALADDIN *adapted*.)

The Queen's new title was celebrated throughout India with great pomp. Here the Queen's Proclamation is being read at Delhi

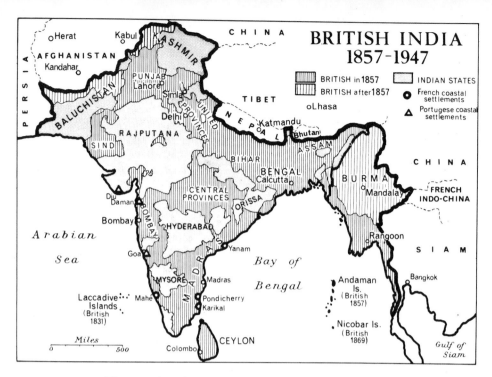

The growth and extent of British power in the sub-continent after the suppression of the Mutiny

questioned: "the army in India was like the London woman who replied, 'No, thank God, we have none of them foul, stinking things here' . . . Bombay, it is true, has a better water supply; but it has no drainage. Calcutta is being drained but it has no water supply. Two of the seats of Government have thus each one half of a sanitary improvement, which halves ought never to be separated. Madras has neither . . . At Agra it is a proof of respectability to have cess-pools. The inhabitants (152,000) generally resort to fields (85)."

Scourge of famine   India was frequently gripped by terrible famines that affected millions of people. Clearly the Raj had to provide famine relief. But many Victorians who believed that charity would undermine self-help, did not want to give too generously. The Famine Commission, set up in 1880, stated that relief should be given so as "not to check the growth of thrift and self-reliance among the people . . . The great object of saving life and giving protection from extreme suffering may not only be as well secured, but in fact will be far better secured, if proper care be taken to prevent the abuse and demoralization which all experience shows to be the consequence of ill-directed and excessive distribution of charitable relief (86)."

Later on, in 1900, Lord Curzon, from the comfort of the viceroyalty, argued that: "In my judgement any government which imperilled the financial position of India in the interests of a prodigal philanthropy would be open to serious criticism. But any government which, by indiscriminate almsgiving, weakened the fibre and demoralized the self-reliance of the population would be guilty of a public crime (87)."

In 1905, after the disastrous famine of 1899–1900, Curzon, who had introduced a new famine policy in 1901, was hopeful about the future: "We may compete and struggle with Nature, we may prepare for her worst assaults, and we may reduce her violence when delivered. Some day perhaps when our railway system has overspread the entire Indian continent, when water storage and irrigation are even further developed, when we have raised the general level of social comfort and prosperity, and when advancing civilization has diffused the lessons of thrift in domestic expenditure and greater self-denial and control, we shall obtain the mastery.

"But that will not be yet. In the meantime the duty of the government has been to profit to the full by the lessons of the latest calamity and to take such precautionary steps over the whole field of possible action as to prepare ourselves to combat the next (88)."

The government also tried to improve India's agricultural *Farming* system. This was literally a matter of life and death, since some seventy per cent of the population were completely dependent upon agriculture. Lord Mayo (Viceroy from 1869–72) expressed the problem in a dispatch: "For generations to come the progress of India in wealth and civilization must be directly dependent on her progress in agriculture . . . There is perhaps no country in the world in which the State has so immediate and direct an interest in agriculture. The Government of India is not only a Government but the chief landlord. The land revenue is derived from that portion of the rent which belongs to the State, and not to individual proprietors. Throughout the

83

greater part of India, every measure for the improvement of the land enhances the value of the property of the State. The duties which in England are performed by a good landlord fall in India in a great measure upon the Government. Speaking generally, the only Indian landlord who can command the requisite capital and knowledge is the State (89)."

Mayo did not want to cause hostility through his agricultural reforms: "In connexion with agriculture we must be careful of two things. First, we must not ostentatiously tell native husbandmen to do things which they have been doing for centuries. Second, we must not tell them to do things which they can't do, and have no means of doing. In either case they will laugh at us, and they will learn to disregard really useful advice when it is given." Mayo went on to admit that he did not know "what is precisely meant by ammoniac manure. If it means guano, superphosphate, or any other artificial product of that kind, we might as well ask the people of India to manure their ground with champagne (90)."

Indian industry was stimulated after 1887 when a modern cotton mill was opened at Nagpur by the Parsee, J. N. Tata. The Tata family were later to build up the Indian iron and steel industry. But until 1911 expansion was mainly limited to the cotton and jute industries as a government report of 1902–3 pointed out: "Nothing illustrates better the present state of industrial development in India than the fact, that after the cotton and jute industries . . . there was only one of the manu-facturing industries . . . namely the iron and brass foundries, in which as many as twenty thousand persons are returned as having been employed during the year. In the preparation of agricultural staples for the market, employment is found for larger numbers; indigo factories . . . employed over 81,000 workers; cotton ginning, cleaning and pressing mills over 65,000; jute presses, 22,000. But of manufacturing industries, properly so-called . . . the most important after cotton and jute mills, are the iron and brass foundries (20,674), silk filatures (10,652), tanneries (8,626), and others of still less importance (91)."

Between 1858 and 1905 the Raj could claim some credit for

economic, legal and educational improvements. But what was the longterm aim of the British in India? Would not the emergence of a class of highly educated Indians mean that these men would call for a greater say in the government of their own country? Eventually India might demand independence! The Victorians could not seriously consider the collapse of the Raj which, until 1905, looked so secure. Lord Curzon put it dramatically when he said, "As long as we rule India we are the greatest power in the world. If we lose it, we shall drop straightaway to a third-rate power (92)." *British aims in India*

The British in India tended to stress that they had a noble mission in ruling a lesser people for their own good. In 1903 Curzon said: "If I thought it were all for nothing, and that you and I, Englishmen, Scotchmen and Irishmen in this country, were simply writing inscriptions on the sand to be washed out by the next tide; if I felt that we were not working here for the good of India in obedience to a higher law and a nobler aim, then I would see the link that holds England and India together severed without a sigh. But it is because I believe in the future of this country and the capacity of our own race to guide it to goals that it has never hitherto attained, that I keep courage and press forward (93)." *Curzon's policy*

But the British did not find all their subjects in India very agreeable. Some British residents found a certain "backward charm" about the impoverished villagers, too concerned with survival to be a political nuisance: "I know the *malgoozar* [headman] of every village, and many of the inhabitants of the knots of hovels scattered over the land. Perhaps 'hovel' is too harsh a name for those snug and sunny mud abodes, with their thatched roofs covered with melons ... What though the mistress of the house labours daily as a coolie for the Biblical price of a sparrow, and carries grain, earth, wood or water on her head, with a high-kilted *saree* [long dress] and inimitable grace, and the master spends his time in sitting aloft in a ... basket, raised on a stick in a ... field, clapping with a wooden clapper ... In short, acting as a scarecrow .. ? Still, when the stone-carrying and parrot scaring are over for the day, many merry talkative parties may be met, returning joyously to bake *An Indian village*

85

Overleaf The British attitude to the Indians was uncertain but the majority of residents no doubt felt that they were there to serve British interests—often literally like the house servants in the photo

the immortal *chupattie* [a sort of pancake] and to feast (94)."

Lord Lytton It was also comforting to argue that the peasantry and the Indian aristocracy were joint upholders of the Raj. Lord Lytton put this point of view in 1877 when he said: "I am convinced that the fundamental mistake of able and experienced Indian officials is a belief that we can hold India securely by what they call good government; that is to say, by improving the condition of the peasant, strictly administering justice, spending immense sums on irrigation works, etc. Politically speaking, the Indian peasantry is an inert mass. If it ever moves at all, it will move in obedience, not to its British benefactors, but to its native chiefs and princes, however tyrannical they may be (95)."

The Babus The most troublesome Indian in the late-Victorian era were the educated *babus*. These men were the products of the system of English education in India, and may well have graduated from Calcutta or Bombay university. They held a very difficult position in society. They had been, in effect, turned into brown Englishmen, but in practice were denied the chance to get the best administrative jobs in their own country. Often they turned their wasted talents to criticism of the Raj. Lord Lytton wrote scornfully of them in 1877: "The only political representatives of native opinion are the *Babus*, whom we have educated to write semi-seditious articles in the native Press, and who really represent nothing but the social anomaly of their own position (96)."

Lord Mayo also had a low opinion of the part the *babus* were playing: "In Bengal, we are educating in English a few hundred *Babus* at great expense to the State. Many of them are well able to pay for themselves and have no other object in learning than to qualify for government employ. In the meantime we have done nothing towards extending knowledge to the million. The *Babus* will never do it. The more education you give them the more they will keep to themselves and make their increased knowledge a means of tyranny (97)."

Opposition to native power The prospect of admitting the *babus*, or indeed any Indians, to a real share of power under the Raj was unthinkable. John Strachey, a member of the Viceroy's Council in the 1860s and 1870s, thought that power could not be entrusted "to the hands

The British did not only go out to India as administrators—the picture
shows a tea planter in front of his bungalow

of Natives, on the assumption that they will always be faithful
and strong supporters of our government. In this there is
nothing offensive or disparaging to the Natives of India. It
simply means that we are foreigners, and that, not only in our
own interests, but because it is our highest duty towards India
itself, we intend to maintain our dominion (98)."

Curzon was much more outspoken. In 1901 he stated that
the strength of his position as Viceroy lay in "the extraordinary
inferiority in character, honesty and capacity of the Indians.
It is often said why not make some prominent native a member
of the Viceroy's Executive Council? The answer is that in the
whole continent there is not an Indian fit for the post (99)."

Of a different tone was an article published by the great
Liberal leader William Ewart Gladstone in 1877. Gladstone
looked more sympathetically at Indian hopes: "The question

*Gladstone: a
Liberal view*

89

Overleaf Although an enlightened minority recognized the demands of
educated Indians to have more say in the running of their country,
the administration was determined not to make any concessions to
people they generally regarded as "inferior"

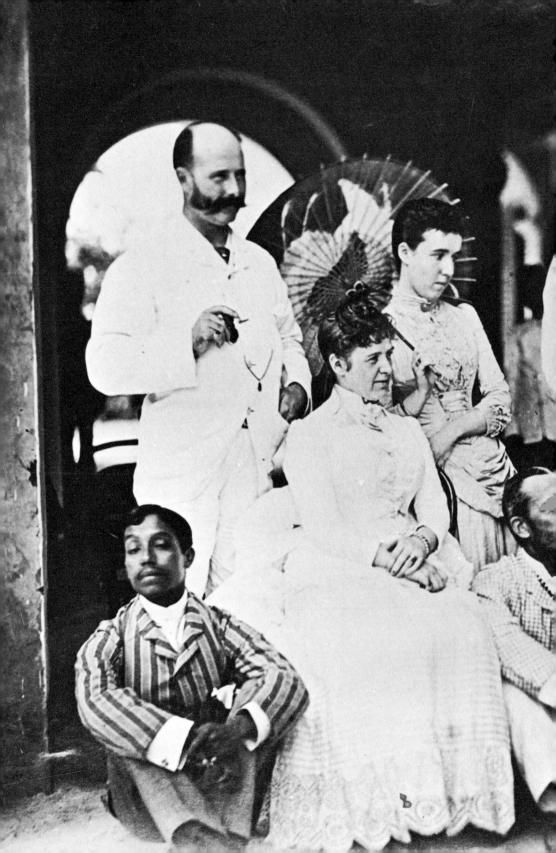

who shall have supreme rule in India is, by the laws of right, an Indian question; and those laws of right are from day to day growing into laws of fact. Our title to be there depends upon a first condition, that our being there is profitable to the Indian nations; and on a second condition, that we can make them see and understand it to be profitable . . . It is high time that these truths pass from the chill elevation of political philosophy into the warmth of contact with daily life; that they take their place in the working rules, and that they limit the daily practice, of the agents of our power . . . For unless they do, we shall not be prepared to meet an inevitable future. We shall not be able to confront the growth of the Indian mind under the very active processes of education which we have ourselves introduced (100)."

Ilbert Bill defeated   Gladstone's high principles were by no means welcome to the British community in India. Many felt that Indian advancement threatened their high-salaried jobs and their social position. The controversy over the Ilbert Bill in 1883 shows the deep prejudices of many of the British in India. Ilbert's Bill proposed that, since many Indians were becoming qualified to act as magistrates, they should be allowed to practise as such, and to try Europeans brought before them. Many of the British community were incensed at this proposal. One Mrs. Annette Beveridge insisted that the Bill would subject "civilized women [*i.e.* Englishwomen] to the jurisdiction of men who have done little or nothing to redeem the women of their own race, and whose social ideas are still on the outer verge of civilization."

The editor of *Friend of India* even wrote: "Would you like to live in a country where at any moment your wife would be liable to be sentenced on a false charge, the magistrate being a copper-coloured Pagan? (101)" The hysterical reaction to the Ilbert Bill worked. The measure was amended so that Europeans would only be tried by an all-white jury!

There were many other examples of racial prejudice in British India. Some were supposedly humorous, like the newspaper advertisement that read: "WANTED Sweepers, Punkah Coolies, and *Bhisties* [water carriers] for the residents of Saidpur. None but educated Bengali *Babus* who have passed the University

Entrance Examination need apply. Ex-Deputy Magistrates (Bengali) preferred (102)."

Rudyard Kipling, the great poet of Empire, who had long experience of India, published in 1886 a poem which poked fun at the Muslims (103):

Rudyard Kipling

> *O grim and ghastly Mussulman* [Muslim]
> > *Why art thou wailing so?*
> *Is there a pain within thy brain*
> > *Or in thy little toe?*
> *The twilight shades are shutting fast*
> > *The golden gates of day,*
> *Then shut up, too, your hullabaloo—*
> > *Or what's the matter, say?*
>
> *That stern and sombre Mussulman,*
> > *He heeded not my speech,*
> *But raised again his howl of pain,—*
> > *A most unearthly screech!*
> *'He dies!'—I thought, and forthwith rushed*
> > *To aid the wretched man,*
> *When, with a shout, he yell'd—'Get out!*
> > *I'm singing the Koran!'*

On other occasions, the British might simply kick Indians out of their way or cuff their servants about the ears. Wilfrid Blunt, while in India, objected to a British passenger on a train in a station threatening some nearby Indians with a stick. The passenger was indignant "at my venturing to call him to account. It was his affair not mine. Who was I that I should interpose myself between an Englishman and his natural right? (104)" Blunt eventually got the irate gentleman to apologize, which was a rare achievement.

Racial feeling

In fact, the British observer or parliamentarian who visited India and dared to criticize the Raj were likely to be even more unpopular than the awkward *babus*. It was assumed that these visitors never understood India at all: "'Mr Cox, the member of Parliament—perhaps you may remember him?' 'A little red-haired fellow, was he? Who wrote a book about India on the back of his two-monthly return ticket?' (105)."

Kipling also wrote bitterly of "Pagett, M.P." (106):

93

The supreme confidence of the British in their own way of life—foxhounds
at Lucknow in 1893

Pagett M. P. was a liar, and a fluent liar therewith,
He spoke of the heat of India as 'The Asian Solar Myth';
Came on a four months' visit to 'study the East' in November,
And I got him to make an agreement vowing to stay till September.

April began with the punkah, coolies, and prickly heat,
Pagett was dear to mosquitoes, sandflies found him a treat.
He grew speckled and lumpy—hammered, I grieve to say,
Aryan brothers who fanned him, in an illiberal way.

July was a trifle unhealthy,—Pagett was ill with fear,
Called it the 'Cholera Morbus', hinted that life was dear.
He babbled of 'Eastern exile', and mentioned his home with tears;
But I hadn't seen my children for close upon seven years.

We reached a hundred and twenty once in the Court at noon,
(I've mentioned that Pagett was portly) Pagett went off in a swoon.

That was the end to the business. Pagett, the perjured fled
With a practical, working knowledge of 'Solar Myths' in his head.

And I laughed as I drove from the station, but the mirth died out
*   on my lips*
As I thought of the fools like Pagett who write of their 'Eastern trips',
And the sneers of the travelled idiots who duly misgovern the land,
And I prayed to the Lord to deliver another one into my hand.

The scorching sun that sent Pagett M.P. running for home *"Prickly heat"*
shone equally fiercely on those who upheld the Raj. "Prickly
heat" was described as "a sort of rash which breaks out on you,
and, as its name infers, is prickly in its nature. I can only com-
pare it to lying in a state of nudity on a horse hair sofa, rather
worn, and with the prickles of the horse hair very much exposed,
and with other horse hair sofas above you, and all around,
tucking you in. Sitting on thorns would be agreeable by
comparison, the infliction in that case being local (107)."

Even without "prickly heat" it was best to shelter from the *The heat of*
sun between midday and two o'clock in the afternoon: "The *day*
white sunlight lies upon the roads in so palpable a heat that it
might be peeled off: the bare blinding walls, surcharged with
heat, refuse to soak in any more . . . In the dusty hollows of the
roadside the pariah dogs lie sweltering in dry heat. Beneath the
trees sit the crows, their beaks agape. The buffaloes are wallow-
ing in the shrunken mud-holes, but not a human being is
abroad of his own will (108)."

When the weather became cooler, or in the evenings, it was
possible to enjoy a promenade in a respectable part of town, to
listen to the military music being played in the bandstand, to
admire the red poinsettias (a tropical flower). One could go to
friends for dinner, or perhaps to an official reception. When
the rains came, the garden would sprout overnight, the roof
might leak . . . and cockroaches and snakes invade the verandah.

But the heat was generally considered worse than the *The hill*
monsoon rains. In the hot season, those families who could *stations*
afford it went to the hill stations (which were like holiday
resorts). Here the air was crisp and cool, and diseases like
cholera were kept at bay. The most famous hill station was

Simla, where the Viceroy and his retinue came to escape from Calcutta's feverish heat. Simla, and other hill stations, soon acquired the reputation for a vigorous social life and adulterous liaisons.

First, however, the women and children had to travel from the plains to the hills. This is how it was proposed to transport a typical family consisting of a mother, three or four children, and a nurse (*ayah*):

> "*1st camel load:* Two large trunks and two smaller ones with clothing.
>
> *2nd camel load:* One large trunk containing children's clothing, plate chest, three bags, and one bonnet-box.
>
> *3rd camel load:* Three boxes of books, one box containing folding chairs, light tin box with clothing.
>
> *4th camel load:* Four cases of stores, four cane chairs, saddle-stand, mackintosh sheets.
>
> *5th camel load:* One chest of drawers, two iron cots, tea table, pans for washing up.
>
> *6th camel load:* Second chest of drawers, screen, lamps, lanterns, hanging wardrobes.
>
> *7th camel load:* Two boxes containing house linen, two casks containing ornaments, ice-pails, door mats.
>
> *8th camel load:* Three casks of crockery, another cask containing ornaments, filter, pardah (purdah) bamboos, tennis poles.
>
> *9th camel load:* Hot case, milk safe, baby's tub and stand, sewing-machine, fender and irons, water cans, pitchers.
>
> *10th camel load:* Three boxes containing saddlery, kitchen utensils, carpets.
>
> *11th camel load:* Two boxes containing drawing room sundries, servants' coats, iron bath, cheval glass, plate basket."

"Or the above articles could be loaded on four country carts, each with three or four bullocks for the up hill journey . . . A piano, where carts can be used, requires a cart to itself, and should be swung to avoid being injured by jolting. If the road is only a camel road, the piano must be carried by coolies, of whom fourteen or sixteen will be needed . . . When a march is made by stages, and one's own cows accompany, these latter should start, after being milked, the night before the family (109)."

Opposite The British in India, 1877. India provided the Victorians with an ideal outlet for commercial expansion and moral endeavour

Overleaf British settlers brought vast quantities of furniture and domestic equipment with them from England so that they could set up Victorian homes in their adopted land

The menfolk, when they could not holiday with their families, carried on the work of the Raj. This is a description of the life of a young judge in a remote district: "Here is Tom, in his thirty-first year, in charge of a population as numerous as that of England in the reign of Elizabeth. His Burghley [Elizabeth's chief adviser] is a joint magistrate of eight-and-twenty, and his Walsingham [another of the Queen's councillors] an assistant magistrate who took his degree at Christ Church within the last fifteen months. These, with two or three superintendents of police, and last, but by no means least, a judge who in rank and amount of salary stands to Tom in the position which the Lord Chancellor holds to the Prime Minister, are the only English officials in a province one hundred and twenty miles by seventy . . . he rises at daybreak, and goes straight from his bed to the saddle. Then off he gallops across fields bright with dew to visit the scene of the late robbery; or to see with his own eyes whether the crops of the *zemindar* [landlord] who is so unpunctual with his assessment have really failed; or to watch with fond parental care the progress of his pet embankment (110)."

The Army, too, had its essential, and not always pleasant, part to play. Disease and drink and debauchery were the lot of the common soldier. But mostly it was a hard slog (111):

> *We're marchin' on relief over Inja's coral strand,*
> *Eight 'undred fighting Englishmen, the Colonel, and the Band;*
> *Ho! Get away you bullock man, you've 'eard the bugle blowed,*
> *There's a regiment a-coming down the Grand Trunk Road;*
> *With its best foot first*
> *And the road a-sliding past,*
> *An' every bloomin' campin'-ground exactly like the last.*

The Indian Civil Service and the Army: these were the twin pillars that upheld the stately structure of the Raj. As the twentieth century opened, they seemed part of a permanent and almost divine order. In fact, the Raj was less than fifty years away from total collapse and disintegration.

6 Towards Independence, 1905–47

LORD CURZON resigned as Viceroy in 1905. He had failed in his self-appointed task of binding the Indian people even more closely to Britain. In a way, therefore, all his reforming zeal had been wasted. More than this, before he left he had sanctioned the partition of the ancient province of Bengal. This move, which was supposed to make the administration of Bengal easier, aroused violent hostility among the Bengali people. The outcry in Bengal, which contained some of the best-educated and most politically-aware citizens in all India, was taken up by nationalist leaders throughout the land.

Trouble in Bengal

Nationalist agitation, or demands for Indian independence, had not been a feature of the Victorian Raj after the Mutiny. Educated Indians voiced certain complaints—for example over the problem of getting into the top levels of the Indian Civil Service. But there was no general call for independence. Even when the Indian National Congress was set up in 1885 it did not seem a real threat. Indeed, there had been strong British support for this annual meeting of academics, landlords, journalists and doctors. The Congress was supposed to allow Indians to let off a little steam, and so prevent a more serious clash.

Indian National Congress

Curzon, typically, had dismissed the Congress in 1900 as "tottering to its fall." But he left India with Congress more active and effective than at any time in its history. From 1905 to 1947, when the British left India, Indian nationalism was alive and kicking, and making steady progress. Faced with this new pressure, the British tried to rally the loyal and conservative elements in the country: the princes, who had so much to lose if the Raj collapsed, the landlord class, and some of the rising industrialists.

Morley-Minto
Reforms
(1909)
But they were forced to make more and more concessions to Indian nationalism. Each concession was meant to buy more time for the Raj. In 1909 the Morley-Minto Reforms were introduced. Named after the Liberal Secretary of State for India, John Morley, and the Viceroy, Lord Minto (1905–10), these reforms had two features. First, one Indian was admitted to the Viceroy's Executive Council (the Cabinet of the government of India), and an Indian was appointed to each of the Councils of the provincial governors. Second, more Indians were to be elected to the provincial Legislative Councils, and these bodies were to be allowed more power to alter laws brought before them.

These measures produced a storm of criticism from the British community in India, and from conservative opinion at home. King Edward VII and the Prince of Wales (the future George V) were hostile. So was much of the press, and the Conservative Party. Arthur Balfour, the Leader of the Conservative Opposition, spoke against giving Indians a majority on the Legislative Councils in 1909: "British administration, good or bad, lacking or not lacking sympathy with native feelings in all directions, is at all events an honest administration sincerely desirous of protecting the poor and the masses of the community by stopping corruption and oppression, which are too common in all countries, and which are the special and poisonous growth of Oriental despotism. Such a government [*i.e.* the Raj] you do not want to control by these . . . majorities, because to control them in that way prevents them carrying out their duties impartially (112)."

Massacre at
Amritsar
The Morley-Minto Reforms did not, as the pessimists forecast, bring about a collapse of the Indian Empire. Indeed, during the First World War (1914–18) India was a pillar of strength in the allied cause. Partly to reward this invaluable loyalty, and partly from conviction, the British government introduced the Montagu-Chelmsford Reforms in 1919. These were the joint work of Edwin Montagu (Liberal Secretary of

EXIT LORD CURZON !

SPEEDING THE PARTING VICEROY;

WELCOMING THE NEW.

ADDRESS OF THE CHAMBER OF COMMERCE.

THE "TIMES" ON LORD CURZON'S SPEECH.

[THROUGH REUTER'S AGENCY.]

LONDON, Nov. 18.

The "Times" dwells upon the great services rendered in the past, and the fair promise in the future to India through Lord Curzon's efforts, but deprecates his allusion, in his Byculla speech, to the controversy which resulted in his resignation. "It may be," the "Times" says, "that Lord Curzon has the support of most of the Indian Army, but can it be supposed that this declaration will smooth the path for Lord Minto ? It does not seem to us that the words, which impair Lord Kitchener's position as head of the Army, can easily be justified."

Probably never within living history has Bombay witnessed such a continuous round of Royal and Viceregal junketings as during the last week or so. What with the coming of the Heir-Apparent of the Empire and his admired Princess, and the round of ceremonies which had been deferred until they could be graced by the Royal presence, and the exit of one Viceroy and the advent of another, Bombay has been more or less in a state of turmoil ever since the good ship "Renown" was sighted in the Harbour. Now things well begin to quiet down; business, (or the business of pleasure) will once more absorb the citizens of Bombay and life in the Gate of India will resume its normal but now very acceptable monotony.

But of all the items in the Royal and Viceregal pageantry which have occupied our minds during the past few days, probably the last to fade from the memory will be the speeding of the parting Viceroy and the welcoming of the new. Both men are "great" in their way. Lord Curzon, the man of ideas, with a bent for reform ; Lord Minto, the disciplined diplomat, whose secret determination is probably to " hold the balance " between opposing parties and to steer clear of interference in affairs which he cannot hope to successfully advance. These differences in the two men were more or less obvious as they walked about beneath the Shamiana at the Apollo Bunder on Saturday morning. Lord Curzon, the born politician backed by Lady Curzon—the prettiest of

while in the second carriage were Their Excellencies Lady Curzon and Lady Minto. His Excellency Lord Lamington left Government House for the Apollo Bunder, from the upper gate, a quarter of an hour before the procession started. On leaving the lower gate the procession passed over Walkeshwar Road, on to the Chowpati seaface along which the drive was exceedingly cool and pleasant. Curving into Churney Road, the pace slackened for some distance. Every verandah and window of the Wilson College which is situated on this road was occupied, while the crowd here was again intense. At the Charni Road level crossing the local traffic of the B. B. and C. I. Railway was blocked for some time, to allow of the procession to pass without any hindrance. Near the Adamje Peerbhoy Sanitarium there was another gaping group of way-farers. While skirting the Hindu burning ground in the vicinity of the Sanitarium, a Jemadar of the Cavalry escort was thrown off his mount, and a few others of the escort fell out to render assistance. Fortunately, the native officer escaped unhurt, and was promptly up on his mount again and with the procession in a few seconds. Leaving Queen's Road, the procession turned into Princess street where His Excellency, the new Viceroy, had the early opportunity of seeing the great recent work of the Bombay City Improvement Trust. The cortege curved sharply into Kalbadevi road which was thronged with natives. As a rule this locality is a crowded one, but on Saturday morning was tenfold so. Cruickshank Road was passed and the procession entered Esplanade Road and drove on at a rapid pace past the Queen's Statue and on to the Floral Fountain, having skirted which the cortege proceeded along Esplanade Road where some of the buildings and shops still had their facings decked, evidently left so till the new Viceroy leaves Bombay. Turning by the Wellington Fountain, the cortege went into the Apollo Bunder road, along which the verandahs and windows of all the buildings there were occupied. No halt was made along the whole route to the Bunder.

THE VICEROY DESIGNATE.

BOMBAY'S WELCOME.

THE NEW VICEROY.

As the steam launch "Bee," with Lord and Lady Curzon on board left the landing stage for the " Dufferin," Lord and Lady Minto for some

Lord Curzon resigned in 1905 having largely failed to achieve his aim of drawing India and the Indians closer to Britain

Visit of the Prince of Wales (later George V) to India. He was among those in Britain who at first opposed making any concessions to Indian nationalism

State for India) and Lord Chelmsford, the Viceroy (1916–21).

The reforms were put into effect by the Government of India Act of 1919. The main points were that the Viceroy's Executive Council should now consist of four British and three Indians. There were a majority of elected Indian members on the Central Legislative Council, and big majorities in the provincial parliaments. Equally important, ministerial posts in the provincial governments were divided between Indians and British. Although Indian ministers were given the "safer" jobs, those that involved hardly any threat to British supremacy, they were at least holding office in their own land. This system of dyarchy, or dual rule, might have been the foundation from which India could have advanced peacefully to Dominion status within the British Empire, as Canada and New Zealand had done. But events were to prove otherwise.

1919 was also the year in which Indian opinion became tragically disillusioned with the Raj. The tragedy came at

Mahatma
104 *Gandhi*

Amritsar in the Punjab where General Dyer ordered his troops to fire on a crowd of demonstrators, killing over four hundred and wounding more than a thousand. Until Amritsar, the British had been remarkably restrained under nationalist provocation. True, in 1908 the Allahabad *Pioneer* had argued that: "The wholesale arrest of the acknowledged terrorists in a city or district coupled with an intimation that at any repetition of the offence ten of them would be shot for every life sacrificed, would soon put down the practice of throwing bombs (113)."

A Commission of Inquiry reprimanded Dyer for his action at Amritsar. It condemned the public floggings for such offences as "the contravention of the curfew order, failure to *salaam* [bow] to a commissioned officer, for disrespect to a European, for taking a commandeered car without leave, or refusal to sell milk, and for similar contraventions (114)."

But many British in India, as well as at home, welcomed the strong hand shown at Amritsar: "Organized revolt is amenable only to the ultimate argument of force. Nothing, now, would serve but strong action, and the compelling power of martial law . . . At Amritsar strong action had already been taken . . . The sobering effect of it spread in widening circles, bringing relief to thousands of both races (115)."

Later in the same book an observer writes from Lahore: "No more trouble here or Amritsar . . . Martial law arrangements are being carried through to admiration . . . and in no time the poor deluded beggars in the city were shouting—'Martial law *ki jai!*' ('Long live martial law!')—as fervently as ever they shouted for Gandhi and Co. One of my fellows said to me: 'Our people don't understand this new talk of *Committee ki raj* (government by Committee) and *Dyarchy raj*. Too many orders make confusion. But they understand *Hukm ki raj* (government by order). In fact, it's the general opinion that prompt action in the Punjab has fairly well steadied India—for the present at least (116)."

Indian leaders did not see things in the same way. Among those who now believed that the British must be driven from India was Mahatma Gandhi. This remarkable man now proceeded to mobilize the Indian masses against the Raj.

Civil disobedience

The magistrates' camp at Amritsar where General Dyer put down
nationalist disturbances with great severity in 1919

Forsaking his westernized style of life (he had qualified as a
barrister in Britain) Gandhi tried to appeal to the Indian people
through a campaign of non-violent civil disobedience.

Civil disobedience meant refusing to pay taxes, obstructing
the progress of the law and the administration, even lying down
on roads and railways. By 1935 Gandhi and the Congress
movement had achieved such success, despite many set-backs,
that the British government passed a new Government of
India Act in the same year. The Act of 1935 effectively created
Indian home rule in the provinces. The Raj was now clearly
under notice to quit.

Toward   The Second World War formed an artificial interval between
independence the Act of 1935 and the achievement of Indian independence.

Congress went into outright defiance of Britain's automatic involvement of India in the war. The Churchill Coalition government in Britain (1940–45) had no option but to commit itself to granting India self-rule as soon as possible. The war was not considered a suitable time for such an historic step, which had to wait until Clement Attlee's Labour government of 1945–51.

Events during the war, however, were drastically to affect the nature of India's independence. In 1942 Congress, led by Gandhi and the astute Jawarhalal Nehru, passed a motion demanding that Britain "Quit India". The Congress leadership was subsequently imprisoned. In the confusion, Ali Jinnah's Muslim League made great headway among Muslim Indians. Jinnah played on the age-old fears of India's Muslim minority. When peace came the Muslim League had won over the vast majority of Indian followers of Islam to the idea of a partitioned sub-continent.

India and Pakistan

Thus when Lord Mountbatten went to India as the last Viceroy in 1947 he had no choice but to divide the old Indian Empire in two—the mainly Hindu state of India on the one hand, and the mainly Muslim state of Pakistan on the other. Burma achieved a separate independence outside the Commonwealth of Nations. The partition of India brought terrible massacres of Hindu against Muslim. Within a year Gandhi was shot dead by a Hindu fanatic who thought he was too lenient toward the Muslims. The two new states were thus born in a welter of blood and conflict. Their future relationship was to be equally stormy.

Westernized Indians

During the half century of the Raj's decline and fall, the British in India mainly pursued their traditional tasks of high-minded administration and profitable business. But there were growing doubts about the purpose of British rule, especially as Gandhi's mass movement made its impact. It was not only the British who expressed their doubts. Some educated Indians found themselves torn between their nationalist convictions and the veneer of British culture that they had absorbed: "I was picked out of the garbage and taken to school—and that was done by the detestable British . . . the Imperialistic British,

Mahatma Gandhi, who led the non-violent resistance to British rule in India, with Sir Stafford Cripps in Delhi in 1942

who bothered to take up a gutter-boy and give him life. Am I grateful? I need not be so very. The British have a passion for alteration. I was educated at the Slane Memorial Scottish School for Orphan Boys. They had my mind and my body for seven years, and for seven years I learned to keep my heart shut away in darkness and starvation (117)."

British observers were also conscious of this dilemma: "You take these boys to England. You train them in the ways of the West, the ideas of the West, and then you send them back again to the East, to rule over Eastern people, according to Eastern ideas, and you think all is well. I tell you . . . it's sheer lunacy . . . You have to look at the man as he will be, the hybrid mixture of East and West . . . You take these boys, you give them Oxford, a season in London . . . You show them Paris. You give them opportunities of enjoyments, such as no other age, no other place affords—has ever afforded. You give them, for a short while, a life of colour, of swift crowding hours of pleasure, and then you send them back—to settle down in their native States, and obey the orders of the Resident. Do you think they will be content? Do you think they will have their hearts in their work, in their humdrum life, in their elaborate ceremonies? . . . In England he is treated as an *equal*. Here, in spite of his ceremonies, he is an inferior, and will and must be so . . . Will he be content with a wife of his own people? He is already a stranger among his own folk. He will eat out his heart with bitterness and jealousy (118)."

This bitterness and jealousy was sometimes caused by Britain's alleged coldness towards India: "We Hindus are hard political bargainers on the surface, but underneath we're eager to be friendly human beings. Mother India never fails to respond to strangers who touch her heart, holding a flame of love and understanding to her imagination. A few English men and women . . . will always be welcome here. The rest of you we only endure because we must. You've patronized and bossed us for two centuries (119)."

Even in the twentieth century it was possible to face ridicule among the British community by asking for greater social contact with Indians. Perhaps this great gulf was maintained largely by the British women in India. E. M. Forster, in his celebrated novel *A Passage to India*, puts this situation well: "She [Miss Quested] became the centre of an amused group of ladies. One said, 'Wanting to see Indians! How new that sounds!' A third, more serious, said, 'Let me explain. Natives don't respect one any more after meeting one, you see.' 'That occurs after so many meetings.' But the lady, entirely stupid and friendly, continued. 'What I mean is . . . I was a nurse in a Native State. One's only hope was to hold sternly aloof.' 'Even from one's patient?' 'Why, the kindest thing one can do to a native is to let him die,' said Mrs. Callendar. 'How if he went to heaven?' asked Mrs. Moore, with a gentle but crooked smile. 'He can go where he likes so long as he doesn't come near me. They give me the creeps.' 'As a matter of fact I have

"A Passage to India"

109

Overleaf "Gandhi Day Parade" in Delhi in 1922 when supporters of Gandhi, released from prison after acts of civil disobedience, marched round the city rallying support

thought what you were saying about heaven, and that is why I am against Missionaries,' said the lady who had been a nurse. 'I am all for Chaplains, but all against Missionaries. (120)''

It was still fashionable to see the Indians as wayward children needing firm handling: "Stacy Burlestone was by nature essentially and fundamentally a kindly man; but long residence in the East and a wide experience of Orientals had led him to the conclusion, right or wrong, that, to the Eastern mind, kindness and weakness are synonymous ... He knew that the Indians' mental attitude towards the kindly and easy European is inevitably tinged with contempt; and that his translation of 'kind' is a word indistinguishable from 'soft' (121).''

Even a cholera epidemic could be mastered by a stiff upper lip: "Towards dawn the men came to us, a great company of them though as you knowest, sahib, it is against the Queen's Regulations for sepoys to come to their officers in crowds, but see thou!—these were no longer soldiers: they were little children lost at night in the great bazaar, and crying for their parents. And they stood before Pollok Sahib and wailed and made obeisance and cried out together—Send for the Colonel Sahib! He will take this torment from us. He will not let this thing be. It will not pass till he returns. But when he comes it will fly away for fear because of his great anger when he sees the evil it has wrought his children (122).''

Public School tradition The public schoolboy who (by and large) manned the administration, the Sandhurst cadet who officered the army, could be variously described. One version portrays them as a self-confident, rather casual, breed: "The much-abused public school product *in excelsis*. No parade of brains or force; revelling in understatement; but they've got guts, those boys, and a fine sense of responsibility ... They're no thinkers, but they're born improvizers and administrators. They've just sauntered down the ages, impervious to darts of criticism or hate or jealousy (123).''

Or again as strong willed, old-fashioned patriots: "Even in an age given over to the marketable commodity, England can still breed men of this quality. Not often in her cities, where individual aspiration and character are cramped, warped,

112

deadened by the brute force of money, the complex mechanism of modern life but in unconsidered corners of her Empire, in the vast spaces and comparative isolation, where old-fashioned patriotism takes the place of party politics, and where, alone, strong natures can grow up in their own way.

"It is to [those men] of an earlier day, that we are indebted for the sturdy loyalty of our Punjab and Frontier troops. India may have been won by the sword, but it has been held mainly by individual strength of purpose, capacity for sympathy, and devotion to the interests of those we govern. When we fail in these, and not till then will power pass out of our hands ... Perhaps only those who have had close dealings with the British officer in time of action or emergency realize, to the full, the effective qualities hidden under a careless or conventional exterior—the vital force, the pluck, endurance, and irrepressible spirit of enterprise, which it has been aptly said, make him, at his best, the most romantic figure of our modern time (124)."

The novelist and essayist George Orwell, who served for a time in the Burma police, gives the other, less flattering version of the servants of the Raj. Like the British officer who "had come out to India in a British cavalry regiment, and exchanged into the Indian Army because it was cheaper and left him greater freedom for polo. After two years his debts were so enormous that he entered the Burma Military Police, in which it was notoriously possible to save money. However, he detested Burma—it is no country for a horseman—and he had already applied to go back to his regiment ... He knew the society of those small Burma stations—a nasty, poodle-faking, horseless riffraff. He despised them.

"They were not the only people whom [he] despised, however. His various contempts would take a long time to catalogue in detail. He despised the entire non-military population of India, a few famous polo players excepted. He despised the entire Army as well, except the cavalry. He despised all Indian regiments, infantry and cavalry alike. It was true that he himself belonged to a native regiment, but that was only for his own convenience. He took no interest in Indians, and his

George Orwell

113

Urdu consisted mainly of swear-words, with all the verbs in the third person singular (125)."

Edward Thompson

Edward Thompson, in *An Indian Day*, described the civil administration equally sharply: "But intellectually the community was third-rate, and its mind was fed on starch and sawdust . . . Administering the myriads evenly and firmly—administering them with an utter lack of perception of what was in the minds of a subject populace and with an unshakable conviction that he was in the place of God and could not err—if you like, doing his magnificent work like a damned fool—but has the world ever seen such glorious damned fools? (126)"

Orwell believed that many British in India hated the worst aspects of the Raj: "All over India there are Englishmen who secretly loathe the system of which they are part; and just occasionally, when they are quite certain of being in the right company, their hidden bitterness overflows. I remember a night I spent on the train with a man in the Educational Service, a stranger to myself whose name I never discovered. It was too hot to sleep and we spent the night in talking. Half an hour's cautious questioning decided each of us that the other was 'safe'; and then for hours, while the train jolted slowly through the pitch-black night, sitting up in our bunks with bottles of beer handy, we damned the British Empire—damned it from the inside, intelligently and intimately. It did us both good. But we had been speaking forbidden things, and in the haggard morning light, when the train crawled into Mandalay, we parted as guiltily as any adulterous couple (127)."

Love-and-hate

As the Raj drew to its end, it was tempting to see the relationship between Britain and India as one of love and hate. E. M. Forster, as early as 1924, saw that a proper dialogue between Briton and Indian could not take place while one was the ruler and the other the ruled. At the end of *A Passage to India*, Fielding, the British liberal, and the Indian, Aziz, ride together, and wrangle about politics. Aziz cried: " 'Down with the English anyhow. That's certain. Clear out, you fellows, double quick . . . We shall drive every blasted Englishman into the sea, and then'—he rode against him furiously—'and then,' he concluded, half kissing him, 'you and I shall be friends.' 'Why

can't we be friends now?' said the other holding him affection-
ately. 'It's what I want. It's what you want.' But the horses
didn't want it—they swerved apart; the earth didn't want it,
sending up rocks through which riders must pass single file;
the temples, the tank, the jail, the palace, the birds, the carrion,
the Guest House, that came into view as they issued from the
gap and saw Mau beneath: they didn't want it, they said in
their hundred voices, 'No, not yet,' and the sky said, 'No, not
here' (128)."

William Buchan, son of the famous novelist John Buchan, Seen as a
love affair
summed up Britain's contact with India in similar terms of love
and hate. What he wrote in *Kumari* could serve as an epitaph
for the British Raj: "The whole thing is and always has been a
love affair. First and last that's been what mattered. And it's
taken the course, worse luck, of most love affairs, beginning
with persuasion—none too gentle in this case—followed by
delighted discovery, mutual esteem, ravishing plans for the
future, the first really frightful row, and a long, miserable
cooling off into polite bickering punctuated by sharp quarrels
and joyless infidelities, each side withdrawing, steadily and
continually, more and more of its real self.

"The first great quarrel, the only one that mattered, was the
Mutiny—that wound went deep and we've never ceased to
suffer, in a way. By then we'd let our character change for the
worse. We'd stopped wooing excitingly, violently, with real
strength and a lot of poetry. We'd grown a great big, bland
evangelical face and were going about doing and saying things
to people—God forgive us—for *their own good* (129)."

Glossary: Some Indian Words

AYAH Nurse or maid

BABUS English-educated Indians

BARGIS Horsemen

BHISTIE Water carrier

BRAHMIN Member of the highest Hindu caste

CHARPOY Simple native bed

CHUPATTIE Sort of pancake

HINDUS Followers of the Hindu religion

KORAN The Bible of the Muslims or Mohammedans

MAHARAJAH Hereditary Indian ruler or prince

MALGOOZAR Village headman

MEMSAHIB Female equivalent of Sahib

MOGUL Name of a great Indian imperial dynasty

MUSLIMS Followers of the Prophet Mohammed

PILAO A rice dish

PUKKAH Fine, splendid

PURDAH The wearing of veils by Muslim women

RAJ Government, or rule

RAJAH Hereditary Indian ruler or prince

SAHIB Sir, Lord

SALAAM A bow, or form of greeting

SAREE Loose robe worn by Indian women

SEPOY Native soldier serving in British Indian Army (especially in the armies of the East India Company)

SUTTEE Hindu practice of burning widows alive on the same funeral pyre as their dead husbands

THUGEE, THUGS The Thugs were a band of robbers who strangled their victims as a sacrifice to the goddess Kali

UNTOUCHABLE Member of the lowest Hindu caste

ZEMINDAR Village landlord

Table of Dates

1784	William Pitt's India Act sets up Indian Board of Control
1788	Impeachment of Warren Hastings on charges of corruption
1795	Warren Hastings acquitted, but ruined
1818	End of Maratha Wars
1824–26	First Burma War
1829	Suttee (widow burning) abolished in Bengal
1839–42	First Afghan War
1843	British conquest of Sind
1845–46	First Sikh War
1848–49	Second Sikh War; British annex the Punjab
1852	Second Burma War
1853	British annex Nagpur
1856	British annex Oudh
1857–58	The Indian Mutiny
1858	British Government assumes sole rule of India; the Governor-General is renamed the Viceroy
1877	Queen Victoria proclaimed Empress of India
1885	Creation of the Indian National Congress
1898–1905	Lord Curzon is Viceroy of India
1901	Death of Queen Victoria
1909	The Morley-Minto Reforms give Indians more power
1914–18	The First World War
1919	The Montagu-Chelmsford Reforms lead to the passing of the India Act of the same year, increasing Indian political power
1919	Massacre at Amritsar
1935	Government of India Act, following Gandhi's civil disobedience campaign, gives home rule to the Indian provinces
1939–45	The Second World War
1947	Lord Mountbatten of Burma becomes the last Viceroy of India; the Indian Empire is divided into two separate states; India and Pakistan become independent, though members of the Commonwealth; Burma leaves the Commonwealth

Further Reading

Bearce, G. D., British Attitudes Towards India 1784–1858 (London, 1961; Toronto, 1961)

Brown, H., The Sahibs (London, 1948)

Davies, A. M., Clive of Plassey (London, 1939; New York, 1939)

Edwardes, M., British India (London, 1967; New York, 1968)
Bound to Exile (London, 1969; New York, 1970)
Glorious Sahibs (London, 1968; New York, 1969)

Feiling, K., Warren Hastings (London, 1954; Hamden Conn., 1967)

Furber, H., John Company at Work (London, 1970; New York, 1970)

Gandhi, M., An Autobiography (London, 1949; Boston Mass., 1957)

Gardner, B., The East India Company (London, 1971; New York, 1972)

Gopal, S., British Policy in India (London, 1965; New York, 1966)

Graham, G. S., A Concise History of the British Empire (London, 1970; New York, 1971)

Greenberger, A. J., The British Image in India (London, 1969; New York, 1969)

Griffiths, P., Modern India (London, 1957; New York, 1965)

Judd, D., The Victorian Empire (London, 1970; New York, 1970)

Pandey, B. N., The Break up of British India (London, 1969; New York, 1969)

Panikkar, K. M., A survey of Indian History (London, 1960; New York, 1966)

121

Philips, C. H., The East India Company (London, 1962; New York, 1961)

Roberts, P. E., History of British India (London, 1952; New York, 1952)

Spear, P., Oxford History of Modern India, Part 3 (London, 1965; New York, 1965) The Nabobs (London, 1963; Gloucester, Mass., 1964) A History of India., Vol. 2 (London, 1965; New York, 1970)

List of Sources

(1) *The Anglo-Saxon Chronicle*

(2) Quoted in Macpherson's *Annals of Commerce.*

(3) Christopher Marlowe, *Tamburlaine the Great.*

(4) Christopher Marlowe, *Faustus.*

(5) John Milton, *Paradise Lost*, book XI.

(6) Quoted in H. G. Rawlinson, *British Beginnings in Western India.*

(7) R. Sencourt, *India in English Literature.*

(8) Quoted in Brian Gardner, *The East India Company* (London, 1971).

(9) *Ibid.*

(10) *Ibid.*

(11) *Ibid.*

(12) *Ibid.*

(13) P. E. Roberts, *History of British India* (Oxford, 1958).

(14) *The Embassy of Sir Thomas Roe*, (Ed. by W. Foster).

(15) *Ibid.*

(16) *Ibid.*

(17) B. Gardner, *The East India Company.*

(18) Letter of Surat Council to Bombay, 1675.

(19) B. Gardner, *The East India Company.*

(20) H. Martyn, *Considerations Upon the East-India Trade.*

(21) From Sir J. Sarkar, *Shivaji.*

(22) East India Company, Letter Book No. 8, 1687.

(23) *Diary of William Hedges* (ed. H. Yule).

(24) India Office Records.

(25) Quoted in Percival Spear, *Modern India 1740–1947* (Oxford, 1965).

(26) J. Law, *A Memoir of the Mogul Empire.*

(27) Quoted in B. Gardner, *The East India Company.*

(28) *Ibid.*

(29) *Ibid.*

(30) *Ibid.*

(31) W. W. Hunter, *Annals of Rural Bengal.*

(32) Quoted in L.S.S. O'Malley, *History of Bengal, Bihar and Orissa under British Rule.*

(33) Charles Grant, *Observations* (1797).

(34) J. Mill, *History of British India* (London, 1820).

(35) Quoted in B. Gardner, *The East India Company.*

(36) *Ibid.*

(37) *Ibid.*

(38) India Office Records, Letter Book No. 14.

(39) *Ibid.* Letter Book No. 15.

(40) *Ibid.* Letter Book No. 17.

(41) *Ibid.* Letter Book No. 15.

(42) *Ibid.* Letter Book No. 17.

(43) Flora Steel, *On the Face of the Waters* (London, 1897).

(44) John Lang, *Wanderings in India* (London, 1859).

(45) Mrs. C. Mackenzie, *Life in the Mission, the Camp, and the Zenana* (London, 1854).

(46) J. W. Kaye, *Peregrine Pultuney, or Life in India* (London, 1844).

(47) *Ibid.*

(48) Mrs. Postans, *Western India in 1838* (London, 1839).

(49) J. C. Maitland, *Letters from Madras By a Lady* (London, 1843).

(50) *Ibid.*

(51) J. H. Stocqueler, *Handbook to India* (London, 1844).

(52) W. H. Sleeman, *Rambles and Recollections of an Indian Official* (London, 1898).

(53) Lady Edwardes, *Memorials of the life and letters of Major-General Sir Herbert B. Edwardes* (London, 1886).

(54) Captain Bellew, *Memoirs of a Griffin* (London, 1843).

(55) Lord Roberts, *Forty One Years in India*

(London, 1898).

(56) J. C. Maitland, *Letters from Madras By a Lady* (London, 1843).

(57) J. Malcolm, *The Political History of India, 1784–1823* (London, 1826).

(58) T. B. Macaulay, *Minute on Education, 1835.*

(59) Quoted in B. B. Majundar, *Indian Political Associations and Reform of the Legislature 1818–1917* (Calcutta, 1965).

(60) J. Pegg, *India's Cries to British Humanity* (London, 1830).

(61) Quoted in M. Edwardes, *British India* (London, 1967).

(62) Sleeman, *Journey Through Oudh* (London, 1858).

(63) *Ibid.*

(64) Quoted in B. Gardner, *The East India Company.*

(65) H. Gough, *Old Memories* (Edinburgh, 1897).

(66) Quoted in Collier, *The Sound of Fury* (London, 1963).

(67) *Ibid.*

(68) Quoted in B. Gardner, *The East India Company.*

(69) *Ibid.*

(70) *Ibid.*

(71) Katherine Bartrum, *A Widow's Reminiscences of Lucknow* (London, 1858).

(72) *Ibid.*

(73) *Ibid.*

(74) *Ibid.*

(75) Quoted in B. Gardner, *The East India Company*

(76) *Ibid.*

(77) George Trevelyan, *The Competition Wallah* (London, 1895).

(78) *Ibid.*

(79) Anon. *Tom Cringle's Letters on Practical Subjects* (Bombay, 1863).

(80) Quoted in B. Gardner, *The East India Company.*

(81) G. B. Malleson, *History of the Indian Mutiny* (London, 1880).

(82) V. Prinseps, *Imperial India* (London, 1879).

(83) *Ibid.*

(84) Lady Betty Balfour, *The History of Lord Lytton's Indian Administration* (London, 1899).

(85) *Observations by Miss Nightingale ... on the Sanitary State of the Army in India* (London, 1863).

(86) Quoted in M. Edwardes, *High Noon of Empire* (London, 1965).

(87) Quoted in M. Edwardes, *British India* (London, 1967).

(88) *Ibid.*

(89) W. Hunter, *Life of the Earl of Mayo* (London, 1875).

(90) *Ibid.*

(91) Moral and Material Progress Report, 1902–3.

(92) Quoted in Denis Judd, *The Victorian Empire* (London, 1970).

(93) Quoted in M. Edwardes, *High Noon of Empire* (London, 1965).

(94) B. M. Croker, *Diana Barrington: a Romance of Central India* (London, 1888).

(95) Quoted in M. Edwardes, *British India* (London, 1967).

(96) *Ibid.*

(97) Quoted in Hunter, *Life of the Earl of Mayo.*

(98) John Strachey, *India* (London, 1888).

(99) Quoted in Denis Judd, *Balfour and the British Empire* (London, 1968).

(100) W. E. Gladstone, article in *Nineteenth Century*, 1877.

(101) *The Englishman*, 1883.

(102) *Ibid.*

(103) Rudyard Kipling, "The Poet's Mistake", from *Departmental Ditties* (1886).

(104) W. S. Blunt, *India Under Ripon* (London, 1909).

(105) Flora Annie Steel, *The Hosts of the Lord* (London, 1900).

(106) Rudyard Kipling, "Pagett M. P."

from the *Definitive Edition of Rudyard Kipling's Verse* (London, 1949).

(107) Lieutenant Majendie, *Up Among the Pandies* (London, 1859).

(108) P. Robinson, *In My Indian Garden* (London, 1884).

(109) S. J. Duncan, *The Simple Adventures of a Memsahib* (London, 1893).

(110) George Trevelyan, *The Competition Wallah* (London, 1895).

(111) Rudyard Kipling, "Route Marchin'", from the *Definitive Edition*.

(112) Quoted in Denis Judd, *Balfour and the British Empire*.

(113) Allahabad *Pioneer*, 5 May 1908.

(114) Quoted in M. Edwardes, *British India*.

(115) M. Diver, *Far to Seek* (London, 1921).

(116) *Ibid*.

(117) R. Godden, *Breakfast with the Nikolides* (London, 1942).

(118) A. E. W. Mason, *The Broken Road* (London, 1907).

(119) D. G. Stoll, *The Dove Found No Rest* (London, 1946).

(120) E. M. Forster, *A Passage to India* (London, 1924).

(121) P. C. Wren, *The Dark Woman* (Philadelphia, 1943).

(122) A. Ollivant, *Old For-Ever* (London, 1923).

(123) M. Diver, *The Singer Passes* (London, 1934).

(124) M. Diver, *The Great Amulet* (New York & London, 1914).

(125) Orwell, *Burmese Days* (London, 1935).

(126) E. Thompson, *An Indian Day* (London, 1927).

(127) George Orwell, *The Road to Wigan Pier* (London, 1937).

(128) E. M. Forster, *A Passage to India*.

(129) W. Buchan, *Kumari* (London, 1955).

Picture Credits

The publishers wish to thank the following for their kind permission to reproduce copyright illustrations on the pages mentioned: The Mansell Collection, *frontispiece*, 10, 13, 16, 17, 20, 21, 26, 28, 30, 31, 32, 34, 38, 45, 47, 48, 79, 80–81, 86–87, 89, 90–91, 94, 97, 104, 106, 108, 110–111; British Printing Corporation, 43, 51, 52, 53, 56, 60, 64–65, 67, 70, 72, 73, 77, 103; Trustees of the Tate Gallery, 68. The map appearing on page 82 is reproduced from Martin Gilbert's *Recent History Atlas* (1966) by the kind permission of the publishers Weidenfeld and Nicolson. All other illustrations appearing in this book are the property of the Wayland Picture Library.

Index